the anti-marketeer's handbook

(or... how to do it all the wrong way and still somehow succeed

adrian liley

"In the land of the blind, the one-eyed man is king."

(Desiderius Erasmus (one of the first postmodernists!) said this back at the beginning of the 16th century, although some say it goes back much further...). It is strangely appropriate to marketing in the early 21st century

and...

"There are few more blood-curdling sights... than books which commence with a quotation from, or allusion to, the work of a distinguished philosopher."

(Professor Stephen Brown – the true 'anti-Christ' of marketing, wrote this at the start of his minor epic: 'Postmodern Marketing' in 1995)

apology of sorts

This handbook is NOT:

- a text book (it is arguably much better than that)
- something that offers any answers
- full of daft questions or tasks at the end of every chapter
- full of rather silly 'case studies'
- crammed with daft words like... synergy, pro-active, cohort or passion
- a place for diagrams, cones, funnels, flow-charts, icebergs or segmented pies
  full of statistics, trends and charts which prove everything and nothing at the same time

This handbook is:

- a trifle (because it is a mixture of odd but satisfyingly nice things)
- a place for telling stories (sorry, I know everyone says this, nowadays)
- a mixture of questionable theories
- about being more than making money
- about contradictions
- a new way of marketing and selling
- about looking at the whole thing from a different angle
- about getting things done by being... nice (most of the time)
-

contents

SECTION FIVE:
The established pillars of postmodernist marketing

SECTION SIX:
Pet hates and Jo Public

SECTION SEVEN:
A vision of an anti-marketing future

SECTION EIGHT:
Anti-marketing in the workplace

SECTION NINE:
Interlude- a look back at how it was

SECTION TEN:
Time to bin a few things

SECTION ELEVEN:
The top ten anti-commandments

SECTION TWELVE:
How to use anti-marketing

SECTION THIRTEEN:
Final Thoughts

introduction
or something
like that

"The highest form of bliss is living with a certain degree of folly."

(Erasmus again – I do like him. And this is my last quote, I promise)

This is the world of anti-marketing or postmodernist marketing – a world where pretty much anything can happen and frequently does. A world where walking away from the deal, helping the customer, recommending competitors, poking fun at your own products and where online games like 'Pokémon Go' matter.

A lot has been said and written about anti or postmodernist marketing – most of it confusing, incomprehensible and contradictory. This handbook is no different. It is also repetitious and superficial when it should be profound and argumentative. If you like SWOT diagrams, the Customer Journey or Boston Matrices, then stop right now. You will be disappointed.

This is a handbook which takes a sly look at the astonishing chaos that modern-day marketing has become, against the backdrop of the English language industry, because that is where I have spent over 30 years teaching, directing, marketing and selling.

It will not try to justify anything, or attempt any grand conclusions, but will try to show you how marketeers are using the full range of anti-marketing materials at their disposal to get their message across, sometimes without even knowing it. Traditional marketing has moved on quite a bit since the advent of the Internet revolution and anti-marketing has become woven into the fabric of modern marketing... whether we like it or not.

There will be no lengthy attempts to talk too seriously about postmodernist meta-narratives or Nietzsche and what 'experts' have attempted to say about postmodernism in the recent past, apart from a few disjointed rambles in the early chapters, which can easily be skipped over.

And, before the purists get annoyed, I deliberately indulge at times in using the words 'anti-marketing' and 'postmodernist marketing', as if they mean exactly the same thing. They probably don't and they probably do. But for me, they do... sometimes.

This handbook is designed to be mildly-amusing, slightly controversial and peppered with daft examples and self-referential parodies, all of which stare into the dark abyss of 21st century marketing with a crazed smile on its face.

But don't let this put you off. It should be a nice ride, packed with contentious comments, ridiculous statements, and superficial explanations. The thrust of the handbook is simply to make you think a little more not just about marketing, but about everything that confronts us nowadays. It is designed to surprise you, when you least expect it.

And... it has the advantage of being extremely 'dippable'. You don't have to read it from page one to get an idea of where it is coming from. Actually, it is probably advisable to open it at any page and have a 5-minute read, maximum. Then stop, go for a brisk walk and throw back something alcoholic.

And, for those readers with limited patience and attention span, there are the pictures – they are there to explain how anti-marketing works in a very practical way on the streets, in shopping centres, on billboards and across the multiverse of the Internet.

There are a few stories too, because this is another facet of anti-marketing. Why? Because people remember a thumping good tale, whereas they will forget page after page of dry theory, with the author desperately trying to sound more intelligent than she/he really is.

There are very few diagrams too, because these are considered by anti-marketeers as the last refuge of the scoundrel attempting to prove something that is difficult to explain in words. There is nothing quite like a cone, spiral, funnel or pie to demonstrate an incredibly daft assertion. Traditional marketeers love diagrams, whilst anti-marketing and 'normal' people just think that an iceberg or a wheel, is just plain silly. Anti-marketeers view most diagrams with disdain, disbelief and dislike.

So, best get one of my own out of the way, immediately. It was attempted in 2015 and stars chaos and hopelessness on a grand scale – it is a mixture of theory and practice, all orbiting total nonsense.

There have been other attempts, especially when a PowerPoint presentation was in the offing, reluctantly constructed so as to explain simple concepts to unbelievers. But none have really measured up or stood the test of time, mainly because such ideas rightly defy categorization. And anyway, as I keep saying, anti-marketing is best when kept well away from diagrams, bubbles, circles, cones or windows.

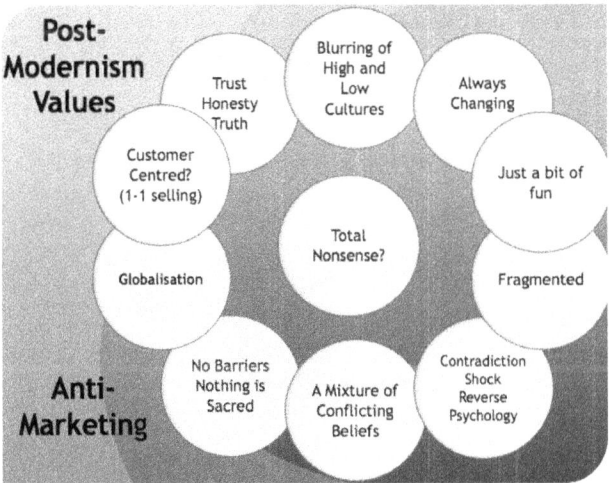

SECTION ONE:

What is anti and postmodernist marketing?

1. here we go

What is anti-marketing?

Well, it's two things. Actually, it could be more, but let's stick to two.

First one: when people with a conscience get together at world trade meetings and throw bricks at anyone from a first world country. There is also lots of tear gas and police with large Perspex riot shields.

Anti-marketing here is a suspicion of the big countries carving up the world's resources to the detriment of all others. It is about people who really hate marketing and everything it has come to stand for in a capitalist world. 'Anti' means 'against' in all its forms.

And that is one meaning. This handbook is not about that, though it does sympathise with the brick throwers, because hurling objects at marketing people is acceptable on so many fronts.

The second is a little more complicated.

And it is not that easy to explain in a few sentences either, because it is a morass of conflicting and contradictory beliefs, which sometimes make no sense at all and only succeed in making you chuckle a bit. Anti-marketing is a riddle wrapped up in a puzzle. It is a slippery beast, which advocates doing all the stuff which surrounds selling in bizarre, odd, ingenious, silly and totally daft ways.

And that's the essence of anti-marketing – it is doing it all the wrong way and somehow getting results. It is breaking the rules and not worrying about what people say. It likes to approach the whole spiky marketing thing from a completely different, oblique, and lateral angle.

There is quite a bit of reverse-psychology, dollops of minimalism, a bit of retro, some storytelling, smatterings of relationship / trust / principled and even accidental marketing, as well as a sprinkling of ethical / green / sacred and evangelical marketing, not forgetting shockvertising, of course. There is also a more sinister side too. Dark marketing is in the mix there, as the villain of the piece.

But it should be emphasised that all this is not… 'anti' marketing.

By that I mean that anti-marketing is not against marketing. It is not a belief that the world would be a better place without marketing. Anti-marketing does not try to attack the concept of marketing, but it simply pokes fun at it, or tries to make the reader, viewer or listener look at it in another way. So, Anti-marketing is not 'anti' marketing. It is far more 'ante' marketing, if you are trying to be extra clever, since all marketeers are encouraged to get a grasp of the lateral stuff long before they start looking at all the things that make up the more serious aspects of traditional marketing.

And this where postmodernism pokes its unkempt head in. You see, anything which smacks of the bizarre in the 21st century is usually labelled postmodernist. It is a convenient cover to wrap all the odd and weird stuff up in – the place where we dump the things we do not really understand and slightly disapprove of.

It really is quite a strange area, because no-one really knows what postmodernism is. This makes it quite hard to nail down, because it has different meanings, depending on whether you are an artist, architect, writer, film-maker or… marketing person.

Renowned professors, extremely-intelligent theorists, writers who want to make a fast buck and even deranged lunatics, have all had a bash at sorting postmodernism out in the past. Some have favoured long lists of bizarre characteristics, whilst others have pushed it into pseudo-scientific silos. Still more, claim it is more an art than a science, where the 'human' element dominates our decision-making over statistics and computerised analytics. A valiant few just say it is a response to a society increasingly dominated by the clutches of the Internet.

And then there is marketing - postmodernist marketing. Some say this can be corralled into a few all-encompassing categories, which always leave the uninitiated gasping in horror and reaching for the dictionary. And so, here they are – the exciting pillars which, according to some experts, hold up the creaking foundations of postmodernist marketing:

De-differentiation
Paradoxical Juxtaposition
'Self-Referentiality'
Fragmentation
Retrospection or Chronology
Hyper-Reality
Parody
Pastiche
Reversal
Centring
Appropriation

Again, don't be put off. Experts always use big words to describe pretty simple things.

So, we will look at all these bewildering areas in the coming pages and will try to work out what they really mean in the 21st century and how they can be applied to practical marketing. We also need to turn over the large stone of anti-foundationalism and will examine all the life existing in these dark, damp regions.

So, postmodern marketing, in a nut-shell, is open to a variety of interpretations which reflect our mood of the moment. It also relies on the public being reasonably clever, tech-literate and generally young. And the emphasis is far more on emotional response. Logic and statistics are not that important.

Postmodernist marketing also encourages customer participation in the whole marketing process. Gone are the days of just marketing and selling to the customer. We are now living in an age of selling and marketing with the customer's help and advice. The customer is on our team. Part of the whole process - on our side of the fence.

And, because the Internet is the dominant factor in our lives, postmodernist marketing involves new areas of segmentation and multiple 'neo-tribes' being created to reflect the customer's online activities.

Finally, there is a lot of fun. Postmodernist marketing rarely takes itself seriously. It loves to poke its tongue out at the customer and at itself. This is usually achieved by irony, parody, pastiche and a general breaking of all the rules out there.

It is a refreshing move from mass marketing to a more individualised way of selling, where each person is important and not just a potential sack of money.

And really finally, the overall emphasis of anti-marketing and postmodernist marketing is offering all customers a complete buying 'experience', where pre and after-sales service are almost more important than the sale itself. After all, a satisfied and happy customer will pass on his or her enthusiasm to other potential buyers. The Internet provides the perfect medium for happy or angry customers spreading their emotions globally.

But before we get too carried away by everything that postmodernist marketing can do for us, let us indulge in the standard anti-marketing technique of explaining things the easy way.

Let's tell a short story. Well, three stories, to be precise.

2. three very short stories

first one

The Etap Marmara Hotel Conference Halls (1st Floor)
Taksim Square
Istanbul, Turkey
October - 1995

It is my first marketing fair. Not the sort of fair where you stand around all day in a tight suit with even tighter shoes, giving out leaflets to bored people wandering around because there is nothing better to do. It is not that sort of fair.

I am sitting down at a table, which is in a long hall with about 100 similar tables arranged in ranks, marching into a neon distance. At each table sits a man or a woman, idly building stacks of glossy brochures, or ripping open cardboard boxes (which contain still more brochures). There is a feeling of worried anticipation in the air.

I am at my table with two brochure trade towers to my right. There is a pad of paper, a pen and a stapler before me. I am young, I am happy, I am excited, I am nervous, I am overdressed and... I am ready. Extremely ready.

"You're doing it all wrong."
"What?"

"That's not the way."

"Isn't it?"

"No."

"Oh?"

"First fair, is it?"

"No," I lie.

There's a long, thoughtful pause. I am not so ready now.

"So, what am I doing wrong?" I have to know.

"Too many brochures out."

"What?"

"When they open the doors, your stuff will disappear quicker than the pile of cakes at a seven-year-olds party."

"What?"

"Just put one on your table. Keep the rest in boxes underneath. Between your legs."

"What?"

"They're not interested in what's in your brochures. Probably couldn't read them anyway."

"My brochure is pretty good and very understandable."

"We all say that… at the beginning. Anyway, it doesn't matter. Not important."

"Really?"

"Tape one to your table. Just one. Tape it down. All four edges and two across the middle, just to make doubley-sure. I would use a staple gun too, but the organisers draw the line at punching holes into the wood below."

I look at my table. I look at his table. One brochure. Taped down. Nothing else. Not even a pen.

"They just look at the pretty colours and then move on."

"What about selling them an English course."

He laughs long and loud.

There is an even longer pause. Now, I'm not happy. To be honest, I'm feeling a bit depressed.

"Then, why are we here?"

"Ah, the biggest question of them all. Do you want the Nietzschian or Wittgensteinian answer?" he smirks.

I say nothing. Back in those days, I probably thought they Nietzsche played for Arsenal or drummed for Pink Floyd. Never mind what Wittgenstein did.

Another long pause.

"And only do the first hour too." He is sitting back in his chair, rocking gently on the two back legs.

"What? Why?"

"Because that's when the organisers are here. Don't say a word. Just stare. And smile. Do nothing."

"What about the students?"

More laughter.

"It's the run up to lunch, then."

"Lunch?"

"Lunch."

"Oh."

"Vital to get to the buffet first. So you don't have to queue for ages. Plus, you get the best choice of food available.   Get in late and you're left with the vegetarian option and none of us wants that. Believe me, I know what I'm talking about."

Three days later. On the plane home.

He passes my seat, having left first class, on his way to the toilet at the back. He stops and turns to me.

"How'd you get on?"

"OK, I think. Longest two days of my life." I chuckle. I'm a veteran now.

"Great."

"And you?"

"Bagged two junior groups for next summer – 25 of the little treasures in each. And 10 adults for next spring, wanting English and Wakeboarding."

"Fantastic," I say, thinly. "I didn't see you on the second day of the fair."

"Didn't bother turning up. Had a long lie in and then went shopping at the bazaar. The wife wanted one of those dreadful Turkish carpets for the front room."

"You went shopping?"

"Yep." He looks up at the overhead bins, where I presume the carpet is stowed.

"So, if you were only at the fair for the first day and said nothing to anyone, how'd you get those groups?" It is his turn to chuckle. "Took the agent who organised the fair out on the first night. Him and his missus. Swanky joint by the Bosphorus. Cost a lot, but got the job done."

"Oh."

Only turned up at the fair on day one to show the flag. Then off like a shot. Hate the things. The secret is to nobble the organisers quickly. And I always do my nobbling in top-quality restaurants, eating fantastic grub and drinking the best wine available on the company credit card."

"I don't understand."

"You will in time."

"So, wining and dining the agent got you the groups?"

"Group."

"I thought you said you had two groups."

"The other was from another agent. A competitor to the first one."

"Great," I say, miserably.

"She's got offices down the road. Met her in the hotel lobby during the fair. Got the group over a very nice bottle of white and a salmon lunch."

"Oh."

"You see, the beauty of successful marketing is not to be seen doing it."

I frown the frown of a young man who wears suits at meetings.

"You'll learn… in time," he repeats and returns to first class.

"What's English and Wakeboarding?" I ask to his back.

"I don't know," comes the distant reply.

"Oh."

He turns at the curtains dividing the rich from the poor and says: "That's the beauty of marketing. No one ever really knows what they're selling…until they're out there on the street."

second one

Norman Park
Bromley
England
February - 2018

I am ankle deep in mud.

"We've got 7 minutes and 20 seconds," says Ash, a mite desperately, staring at his two mobile phones. "Then it despawns." His suit trousers are covered in horse manure splatter. "We can still do it," he mutters and starts jogging down a swampy path, still staring at his phones.

I follow, trying to hop around the muddier bits, not staring at mine. There are limits, although I would never say this out loud and in his presence.

We are on a sodden track at the back of Norman Park - a wide expanse of greenery in Bromley Common in south London, quite near the local football ground and a 'travellers' encampment. It is not the place to be on a bleak, cold, soggy, winter's afternoon.

Ash climbs a rickety wooden gate and leaps into the sanctuary of the park beyond and into another puddle. I smile inanely at two small girls and a damp-looking boy standing in wellingtons in a field next to a grubby horse. Then I follow. A very wet lemming.

A few minutes later and we reach a concrete path.
"3 minutes and 46 seconds left," squeaks Ash, after quickly consulting his phones. "We can still do it!" He runs towards the main road. I follow at a slower pace, age kicking in. We are not going to do it. Any sane person can see that.
"There's a bus!" shouts Ash, as a 208 clanks past. We pick up the pace and jump on board, trousers dripping.

"1 minute and 53 seconds - and then possibly another 30 seconds, after it disappears from the map," gasps Ash. "We can still do it." However…

We have not reckoned on the road-works by the Crowne pub and the extra set of traffic lights… on permanent red.

Time ticks by. We arrive at a stop near a roundabout a few yards away from where the 'it' is lurking – our target and reason for all this haste. Phones are out and we are scanning the area like Kirk on an alien planet. A 'Pidgey' pops up by a letterbox, then a 'Weedle', followed by a 'Murkrow'.

We are hunting Ditto.

Ash is an adult. And probably a responsible and sensible one… in normal circumstances. He has a solid, and some would say, admirable job in social services and also studies hard on courses to improve himself. He is an intelligent, thinking adult. As for me… well, probably none of the above, apart from the adult bit. Actually, I am more post-adult.

We are indulging in the activity of playing (if that is the right word) the online game – *'Pokémon Go'*. Yes, *'Pokémon Go'* – the kids game. Let's get that out of the way first. The kids game. Kids.

And we are not kids, as I have already said. Well, not in the technical sense of the word. But we are playing *'Pokémon Go'*. And playing it seriously, passionately and almost addictively, though we would never admit this.

Our phones are key to the whole experience, since the cartoon monsters we are after, are linked by GPS locations and only 'spawn' for a limited span of time – hence all the muddy hurrying about. We spend our days looking at maps, as they scroll across our screens and hoping that a 'rare' (or 'Hundo', or 'Shundo' - the ultimate prize) will pop up, when we least expect it.

Ash also has another 'App' on his mobile, which tells him where the all good stuff is in Bromley at that particular moment. It is a bit like having an Enigma Machine, devoted to spotting Pokemon creatures, in your pocket. Incidentally, a 'Ditto' is a lilac blob with a daft expression.

I am feeling a little guilty. Not for all the obvious reasons. But because I wasted precious seconds buying £20 worth of gold coins, so I could get my hands on a few egg incubators to capitalise on all this walking around. Mileage is a valuable commodity in this game. And a lot of steps means you hatch your eggs. It is a tricky and complicated business. But buying online coins to get the incubators wasted time back there... before the muddy bits.

We miss the Ditto by about 20 seconds...

... and collapse in the Harvester pub for a pint each and to get ready for the next dash. The barmaid pointedly tells Ash where the toilet is – he is beginning to pong a bit. He disappears for 20 minutes. When he returns, he has got that animated sparkle back and has freshly-scrubbed trouser bottoms. He smells of pub toilet soap.

"There's a Level 5 raid in 40 minutes at the War Memorial," he gushes. "Already 6 accounts confirmed for hatch." He sups hard at his lager and then immerses himself in his phones.

"Shame about the ditto," I say.

"Mmmm," is the reply.

The Ditto is history.

He suddenly goes rigid. "Drink up," he says. "There's an 'Eevee' Hundo in Waitrose car park." He's out of the pub before I can reply.

(just in case you're wondering, a Hundo is a very rare, top level version of a creature out there with 100% ratings on all statistics. A Shundo is even rarer. These are Shiny Hundos - about as easy to catch, as it is to win the lottery. We all want Hundos, but we dream of Shundos. There are also beasts nicknamed 'Shlundos', but to go on about this would hint at being worryingly addicted to the game, so I'll stop right there)

third one

My House
Bromley Common
Bromley
England
March - 2018

I received a promotional video this morning by email. It was from one of my favourite anti-marketing gurus, Seth Godin. This is a man who treads dangerously close to the edge of marketing insanity.

He has just published another book, modestly entitled: *'This is Marketing'*. But never mind the book for now. I am intrigued by his sales method. He has sent me this video to me. To all his 'followers'. His fans. His acolytes. I put headphones on and hit the play button.

He gets straight down to business, talking about all the crazy methods that he has used to sell his wares in the past. It is all very funny and increasingly, mesmerizingly bizarre. You see, Seth likes to be different, cutting-edge and at the forefront of anti-marketing.

He tells me that his first book (*'Purple Cow'*) was sold in a paper milk carton. Yes, a milk carton - one of those with the triangular 'push-open' spouts. His second was encased in a cereal box. His third… you get the picture?

I should point out, at this point, that Seth is completely bald (not that I have anything against follically-challenged males – I am one myself). I mention it, because it somehow seems important in the grand scheme of things. He also has massive, hypnotic glasses and a penetrating stare. He always reminds me of the Disney snake in *'The Jungle Book'*. Kaa. The one who sings: "*Believe in me…*" with wide kaleidoscopic eyes.

Now, don't get me wrong, I like Seth Godin. I like him a lot. I do not mean to call him a snake in a bad way. Of course not. He is brilliant and approaches the whole spiky subject of marketing in a totally unique and very practical manner. Almost cunning, some might say. Snakey.

I have bought several of his books in my time and ploughed through them – cover to cover. They are really good and very readable. But what always amazes me is not what he writes, even though it is pretty good stuff. What I am in total awe of are the methods he uses to sell his books.

Seth knows that the secret to selling is in the packaging. Not the product. Never the product. That is of secondary importance. Sell the cover. It is what we see first and will always be the most important moment in the sales process - that first second when our eyes light on the thing. Seth knows this. *Believe in me…*

The video continues. He juggles on screen with his previous sales successes. He shows us the carton, the cereal box and other stuff. Then we get a brief look at his latest offering: *'This is Marketing'*. This is a very big *'Believe in me…'* moment.

We are told to concentrate on the packaging. Forget about the contents. Who cares about them? Not a mention on what the book is about, though I could probably guess - the title is a bit of a give-away. Seth does not give a monkey's about the pages within.

This is when it all gets a bit clever. Snakey. Seth brandishes a sheet of dust cover mock-ups. Dust covers. Yes, that is right. Dust covers. He is selling us the paper around the book. *Believe in me….* And it is going to be a limited edition. OK, that has been done millions of times before, I hear you mutter, BUT… each book is going to have a randomly-coloured dust cover (from a set of eight). Eight different dust covers. EIGHT!

Now we are getting to the genius bit! Seth looks deep into our eyes and offers us the chance to get ALL eight dust covers – the complete set, at a reduced price! How brilliant is that? He is trying to sell eight copies of the same book on the pretext of owning a different dust cover. Eight! Genius. The implication is that having all eight just might be collectors' item in about a hundred years or so. 'Go out there and make a ruckus!' he says at the end of the video. *Believe in me…*

I sit still staring at the frozen, hypnotic image of Seth's face, my fingers twitching for my MasterCard.

Believe in me…

So, what are these three mini-stories about?

What is the common link? Well, they all have some sort of relevance to anti-marketing or, if you are feeling superior, postmodernist marketing.

The *'Pokémon Go'* tale touches on everything that postmodernism and anti-marketing stands for. It is making money from the unreal. The hyper-real. It is moving around in a digital world (augmented reality, to be precise), where you can experience adventure, relationships, friendships, romance, joy, heartache and even get to spend some real money… on nothing tangible at all.

The story in Istanbul of the salesman who knew how to play the system like a well-tuned violin, shows how you can get business by doing absolutely nothing that marketing textbooks advise. It is playing the 'human' card somewhat brutally and ignoring as many funnels, cones and bar charts as possible. It is about getting the deal by being different.

Finally, there is Seth Godin and his video. This is a master-class on how not to sell your stuff... and yet, still sell your stuff. Seth is an anti-marketing genius – he knows how to be... 'remarkable' (his word and probably patented).

All three have a role to play in this handbook, since they teeter on the edge of superficiality and silliness at times, while trying to tell another story.

And that is what this handbook is all about. It is Nietzsche rubbing shoulders with a 'Jigglypuff'. It is Mel Brooks, Troy Tempest and Professor Stephen Brown all at the anti-marketing dinner table, munching Marmite sandwiches and supping Guinness, while waiting for something to happen. Maybe Godot will arrive or Banksy will spray paint a girl with a balloon on the table.

Whatever happens next, we can be sure that it will be strange, exciting, remarkable and extremely unpredictable.

Drum roll...

3. i hate marketing and selling

I hate marketing. I hate selling even more.

I hate them both. Hate.

I should quickly say that I have just read a book by Steve Morgan (*'Anti-Sell', 2019*), which begins with the same line. I could claim I wrote my hate line long before he did, but what would be the point? He got his into print first. I can only ruefully say that great minds think alike. And, I should quickly add that I thoroughly enjoyed his voyage through these choppy waters.

I should also say, here and now, that I wanted to start this handbook with a bang and could not think of a better way than a few pages raging about my hatred for the very thing that I am going to have a stab at talking about.

I probably should have started with multiple, incomprehensive theoretical layers of postmodernism and why it has any relevance in the marketing arena. But I did not, because I thought that doing it another way would be more interesting. Perhaps doing it this way would hold the attention of the reader that bit longer, although Seth would probably just smirk and say that if you are this far in, then job done. Ruckus made. Kerchink…

This is definitely the moment when you should have a flick through to the middle of the handbook where the pictures start, especially if you are not in the mood for lots of text, which may make you think a little too much and verges on the ridiculous, at times.

For those of you that are left, or have returned here after your foray with the pictures – please reach for a stiff drink and brace yourself. This is going to be bumpy ride.
So, why the hate?

Well, it is all a bit of a mess.

A mess which starts with the names themselves - sales and marketing. And I am talking about all this on a very practical level in my particular little industry. In the past, it was rather simple. Companies saw marketing and sales teams as the sharp end of the organisation. Plan and then sell. Give them all a budget and then push them out the door to sell stuff, marketing and sales working hand-in-hand, existing only to shift products as fast as possible.

And no one really knew where marketing stopped and sales started. Both were intermingled, joined at the hip and pretty much doing the same thing.

So, what are the differences?

An old boss of mine once said, when pushed, that the main distinction was: *'Marketing people sit around all day, while sales people wander the streets.'* You can't really argue with that. Well, you can, but you would most definitely be a marketing or sales person, who had done one too many courses, or walked one too many streets, if you did. Marketing people are usually seen as overpaid vultures, while sales people are viewed as roaming, opportunist scavengers. Both similar types of carrion eaters.

A marketing colleague and friend once said: *'The main difference between the marketing person and the sales person is the salary.'* Again, absolutely true. No problem with that. As true as the sun in the sky.

Some 'experts' claim that it is all pushing and pulling. Sales is the 'push' part of the process, while marketing is the 'pull' part – push meaning harrying potential customers until they buy your stuff and pull meaning building a trap to entice customers with flapping wallets.

Others see marketing as more of a long-term game, which requires strategy, tactics and months of data analysis, while sales is the brutal end of this process where money gets involved. Marketing is all about the 'planning', while sales is the 'doing'.

A few claim that marketing is aimed at the customer, while sales only concentrates on the product. That takes a few moments to think about, but it is quite a neat distinction except that in real life, it does not really work. Sales today is very much about the customer, as well as the product. As for marketing – well, that is aimed at everything in the known universe.

Some claim that marketing is there to help businesses understand what a customer needs and wants, while sales is there to meet those needs and wants. This seems closer to the mark, since it concentrates on a symbiotic relationship between the two. Without one, the other cannot work and vice-versa.

Another one: marketing is all about putting the brand first, then the product and finally person. Sales is different. It is about putting the person first, then the product and finally, the brand. Not sure I agree with that. It is not as simple as grading everything into a simple list of priorities. All are just as vital.

There is more. Marketing is about 'influencing' potential customers to like a product and brand, whereas sales is informing the customer of the 'benefits' of the product over similar products in the marketplace. Very neat, although such a distinction teeters on the brink of unscrupulousness. Influencing people sounds like 'hard-selling', while listing all the reasons why your stuff is better than everything else just will not be believed, nowadays.

More controversially, marketing has, in the past, been defined as mass media, while sales was viewed as being one-to-one. Not really true anymore, but a nice try.

And it has been argued that marketing and sales is like a pipeline with a large funnel at one end and a small exit at the other. You pump all your marketing data into the funnel… and sales pop out the other end. Like squeezing icing onto a cake, or toothpaste onto your brush.

Another nice and very succinct distinction is: in sales, you telephone them; in marketing, they call you. A pithy explanation, which is back to the pull / push thing again.

What about this one? Marketing is about creating 'awareness' and making people want your product. Sales is acting on the want. A nice and tidy distinction, which avoids the heavy influencing.

Probably the most relaxing one is this: marketing is there to make the selling environment easier. It is just a comfort pillow for the sales person to fall back on. I like that one. Anything with pillows is always good.

Traditional marketing is all about pushing, pulling, planning, lots of awareness, influencing, heaps of benefits, needs, wants, pipelines and comfort pillows. It is also aggressively scientific - with consumer ladders, interpretation of mass data, spreadsheets, Sun-Tsu, the mapping of customer journeys, being innovative 'within a given framework' and adhering to the 'marketing mix'. It is about pro-active synergy and talking constantly about the 4, 7 or 12 Ps. It is about product lifecycles, bell-curves and windowed diagrams. And most importantly, it is all about consumer behaviour and how to predict which direction the person in the High Street will jump next.

Just sell, sell, sell!

And as for sales, well… that is about taking the money. Somehow using all those Ps will get customers to throw cash at you. As simple as that.

What follows is a little cruel... It is a sad fact that most sales teams still consist of bright, young things with the 'gift of the gab' and not much else. They are not there to think very much - just to sell. They are recruited, because they showed a bit of 'cleverness' at the interview. Stood out from the rest. Were confident, relaxed and at ease in a stressful situation. And... not much else. And after joining a sales team, there usually is very little practical training. Everything relies on the innate ability of the sales person to bring home the bacon. You either have it or you don't. The good ones sell stuff and the bad ones don't. And on Friday afternoons, the bad ones are fired. It is natural selection on a very speedy and unforgiving scale. Sales people are instantly replaceable and of no real worth, except as a conduit between the customer's wallet and the company's bank account.

Sales teams have always relied on something that is not really definable. Something that cannot be described in any pertinent way. Something that some managers simply call 'the X factor'. We can pretend that there are other factors at play, but what it comes down to is simply that. The person who sparkles and who will fit into the existing team, will get the job, no matter how long the list of qualifications or pages of experience. It is simply a fact of life... and probably always will be.

This is both good and bad. Good obviously because a sales person naturally has to have the gift of the gab and be able to think on his or her feet. Bad because it has nothing to do with theory or beliefs. A sales person is recruited to be a 'talker' and nothing else.

He or she is not there to implement company marketing theories, although technically, he or she probably is. What it all comes down to is whether the sales person can get the sale using whatever means he or she deems necessary at a particular time and place.

Personality is the name of the game here. And no charts have been constructed yet to map out the psychology of the successful sales person. It is still a mystery.

And so, I hate marketing and sales. There is no clear definition of the roles except probably that marketing is about planning, while sales is about the action of taking the customer's money. In today's society, even that distinction is debatable.

With the advent of the Internet and online selling, it could be argued that both marketing and sales are now pretty-much indistinguishable to all intents and purposes, since the online marketing person is involved in the selling, while the sales person is an integral part of the marketing planning. Some have even argued that as we reach the end of the decade, sales and marketing are virtually identical in practical terms.

The sales team can now sit at computer terminals and design their own campaigns, while the marketing team can get involved in the direct selling. Perhaps this the one of the reasons why some companies have rolled it all together into one department with a 'Sales and Marketing Manager' as the person in charge. One person controlling the whole lot.

SECTION TWO:

postmodernism
- the essential
bits for
marketeers

4. a bit of homespun theory

And now... Postmodernism rears its ugly head

This is a book about what I like to call anti-marketing. But, by its very nature, it is not. Well, bits of the handbook certainly are, but in order to understand what the 'anti' thing is all about, we need to tackle a rather large elephant sitting in the corner. Actually, it is probably not an elephant at all, but it most certainly could be. And here we come to the crux of the trunky beast.

Postmodernism and one of its bastard children, postmodernist marketing, are large, moody, unpredictable, puerile pachyderms, out to mess with you, at every possible turn.

But before I approach both beasts with a sack of buns, I should quickly address the problem of the label - postmodernism. We will get to marketing a bit later, but it would seem logical that we should talk about this wobbly entity first.

Let's start with a great quote, which explains it all:

"Postmodernism is a cultural condition and philosophical position associated with postmodernity that questions the fundamental assumptions of modernism. It is closely related to poststructuralism and deconstructionism." (Firat & Venkatech, 1995).

Now, you can see what we are dealing with. Assertions like this sound great, but very few people will actually understand what is being asserted, least of all a sales team out to try something different. What sentences like this do is just raise more questions and generally bamboozle the reader. The meaning though, is not so complicated. It is just an assertion that modernism might have had its day and that postmodernism and postmodernity (subtly different, I can assure you) just might have a few answers up its/their sleeve(s).

Another easier explanation is that postmodernity is the *'attainment of the quest for an individual's liberation'* (Cova and Cova, 2009). Which is a little clearer, although it does sound a little like a line from the Labour Party manifesto.

So… where do we go from here, without backing into a theoretical cul-de-sac? Well, to understand it all a little better, we first need to look at the word… without the post.

So, here we go. Modernism

It has been claimed that modernism is related to *'the rule of reason and the establishment of rational order.'* (Cova,1996). And that really is the essence of the beast. It is the application of logic, reason, science and technology… and the creation and reinforcement of what are called 'metanarratives' or universal truths.

And this pretty-much all happened during the 20th century (that is another simplification, I know) with such movements as Marxism, communism, anarchism and even fascism, fundamentally altering the traditional powerbase, which had existed since time-immemorial, where kings, queens, emperors and royal dynasties ruled and where serfs, slaves, workers and... the common people had very few rights.

Modernism sought to improve the lot of humanity by creating sets of rules, which claimed to have all the answers as to how we should live our lives in communal happiness. For example, Communism and socialism sought to improve the lot of the lower and working classes, while fascism went for the superiority of certain races over all others.

Whatever the doctrines, they all agreed on one thing – that violence, mayhem and death were legitimate ways to carry out their respective visions and that life would be a lot better for all than it had been previously. And people bought into this, mainly because life after the First World War was pretty desperate on all fronts. And anything had to be better than that.

Firat & Venkatech (1995) summarised the thing like this. Modernism was:

1. **the rule of reason**
2. **the establishment of rational order**
3. **the emphasis of science and scientific method**
4. **the application of scientific technology**
5. **the unity of purpose in art & architecture**
6. **the emergence of industrial capitalism**

7. **And finally, it separated 'production' from 'consumption'.**

So, it is law and order on a grand scale. Modernism laid the rules down in all areas and was designed to give a blueprint to society for how to live in collective harmony for the good of all, with lots of absolute truths all over the place. Prosperity and happiness could then walk off into the sunset, hand-in-hand. It advocated a society which was rational, logical, lacking in any emotional commitment and encouraging the belief that if you worked hard, then you would be successful. The idea of happiness did not enter into the equation, since modernism equated work and this kind of limited individuality with being happy.

Enough of that for the time being.

Postmodernists came along in the latter half of the 20th century and started questioning these 'truths' or 'metanarratives' - the core of the debate being simply that they did not work anymore (if they ever did work). Not many people would argue that modernist metanarratives needed a serious looking at after the Second World War, the Holocaust and the dropping of two nuclear bombs.

Human beings, by their nature, are individuals and will eventually rebel against rigid laws and confinement, especially when such metanarratives have had such a massive negative impact on society, despite all the positives. It has also been argued that postmodernism attempted to bring a little magic back into an over-logical and rational world.

Postmodernism is opposed to rational thinking, preferring fragmentation and a total loss of faith in metanarratives. It denies any single utopia or system of beliefs and encourages multiplicity and the growth of many styles and thought processes. It is a complete relaxation of the rigid laws that governed modernism. And in allowing pretty-much everything to blossom without fear or recrimination, it implies disorder and chaos on a grand scale.

It is generally accepted that the theorist – thinker - philosopher, Jean-Francois Lyotard, was one of the first 'experts' to put his finger on the pulse of this growing scepticism, when he wrote his ground-breaking paper, *'The Postmodern Condition'* and posted that famous line that postmodernism was an *'incredulity towards meta-narratives'*, which, in layman's terms, means that Joe Public should not see just one doctrine as an over-riding and all-encompassing answer to society's questions.

The essence of postmodernism is the emphasis on spectacle, image, individuality and humanity over logic, narrative and substance. Time and space are not important anymore. Everything is less stable and deconstructed, even confused and un-unified. The imaginary has become as important as reality. It expounds openness, tolerance and the complete acceptance that people are different politically, religiously and culturally.

Then, of course, came along a few experts who deemed it necessary to draw distinctions between 'modernism' and 'modernity' and, not surprisingly, 'postmodernism' and postmodernity'. Without dwelling too long on this potential ticklish knot of confusion, it is probably an easy way out to say that both modernity and postmodernity relate to social and economic changes in society. Meanwhile, modernism has sometimes been linked to something called 'progressive, revolutionary movements', while postmodernism finds its happy hunting ground where the intellectual, abstract and aesthetic rule. Not surprisingly, Philip Kotler said, quite astutely, that *'panic is the archetypal postmodern state of mind,'* which is a nice way of putting it.

A pipe

Incidentally, just reading Lyotard's essay also underlines another reason why people have very little idea as to what it is all about. Postmodernism is described in dense theoretical language that all but a few can understand or follow. I have tried and failed miserably, probably because I am of limited intelligence, being a man of the people!

So, to make things relatively simple, let's turn our attentions to the world of art and Henri Matisse's painting below.

Why? Because it has huge relevance to modernism and postmodernism – and eventually to marketing, if you are thinking extremely laterally. And because I think it is brilliant picture which asks so many questions.

Anyway, here it is. It is a pipe. Just an ordinary pipe. And not a particularly remarkable painting of a pipe either. And that is about it.

So, why all the fuss?

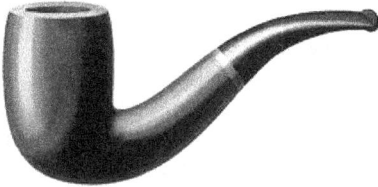

Ceci n'est pas une pipe.

Let's look a little closer. It is a picture of a wooden pipe floating unaided on a sepia background. Underneath is written the somewhat perplexing sentence: *'Ceci n'est pas une pipe.'* (This is not a pipe). Except for the strange negative assertion, it looks like a fairly unremarkable image of a pipe you would probably find in a standard schoolbook.

Lots has been written about Matisse's pipe. Everything from the obvious (the paradox of the negative statement) to the slightly obscure – the gap between 'ceci' and 'n'est' and things called calligrams. Of course, at the centre of the debate, is the assertion that the thing is not a pipe.

Of course, it is.   Not even the most extreme existentialist could claim that this is not a pipe. Surely?

Matisse disagrees. After all, technically this is NOT a pipe. It is merely a representation of a pipe. A picture of one. And you can't smoke the picture! This is Magritte's point. It is an image of a pipe, so technically... it is not a pipe.

Now, I will resist the temptation of drifting into an absorbing discussion on place, text, image and space, all backed up by existentialism. What I will say though, is that the power of the 'word' is extremely important. Our understanding here is essentially linguistic.

Now we have the first of many contradictions. It is also a good starting point in what postmodernists call hyper-reality, since the picture of the pipe does not exist in any tangible, 'pipey' way at all, but is merely a cartoon representation of one. And yet, it is a real pipe in a hyper-real way.

This is where a few problems start, since modernism and postmodernism tend to overlap quite confusingly. Whereas Matisse is essentially modernist, his pipe picture can be interpreted as being extremely postmodernist, because it can be interpreted in a hyper-real, ironic, self-conscious way, filled with parody, ambiguity and even dipping its toe into the absorbing discussion of what high and low culture is.

Some have claimed that postmodernism is just the extension of modernist debate, since it would be foolhardy and pointless to separate the two. Others see postmodernism as a radical next step, a complete break, which amply reflects the new age of communication, art, television, film and the Internet, much better than the static age of modernism.

Whatever it is, it is more playful, controversial and fun. Matisse is having a good chuckle at the confused viewer, much in the same way the Marcel Duchamps probably did at the turn of the 19th century with his urinal. Both the picture of the pipe and the wall-mounted urinal are merely representations of the 'real' thing. Whether they should be seen as art is something else – but cutting edge postmodernism, they certainly are.

Think Roy Lichtenstein, Munch's 'The Scream' and quite a few Picassos, then throw in Frank Gehry's architecture, Andy Warhol, Patrick McGoohan's 'The Prisoner', virtually every episode of 'Seinfeld' and even Scooby Doo. They all get a place at the table!

Then you will have an idea of where postmodernism is coming from. Self-referential mixtures of what was perceived as high and low culture messing with parody, time, humour, silliness, space and… image. The whole lot is thrown into the melting pot and given equal status to reflect where society is at.

Let's look at another aspect. An aspect which I particularly enjoy rambling on about. It is what the philosopher, Wittgenstein and the theorist, Baudrillard, called 'referents', 'representations' and 'simulacra'.

It sort of sums up postmodernism, since it hammers home the Matisse pipe point and leaves you wondering about things which you probably had not thought about before… and regret thinking about now.

So, what are referents, representations and simulacra? What's the story here?

A simple explanation would be to say that a representation is just an 'equivalent' or imitation of the original (the referent). Like a photograph, or a painting, or even a story or television programme about a particular subject. It is our way of describing and discussing the 'original'. And can be enjoyed and appreciated for what it is. But the area is fraught with complications and difficulty.

For example, when we look at an original painting by Picasso or Monet, we marvel at the beauty of the work, but when we look at a copy or a fake, we treat it with disdain, despite the fake probably being of similar beauty and probably indistinguishable from the real picture. Perhaps this is because the imitation has tried to fool us in some way. It is trying to prove that we are stupid. And no one likes to be considered stupid. If, on the other hand, we know we are buying a poster of the Monet or Picasso, then this is all fine and dandy. We know it is a copy and do not feel fooled. Everyone a winner when the truth is out there for all to see. But it gets more complicated.

Television news teams, newspapers and the Internet use their privileged positions to take the referent (the story unfolding in front of the reporter's eyes) and then interpret it the way they want to. The representation then becomes a very subjective entity. It is not fake or a copy, but just a subjective 'opinion' on the reality. It is interpreted through the eyes of the beholder. And we are asked to buy into this version of the truth, because we trust the storyteller.

The writer, Baudrillard, develops the whole referent-representation discussion into the sphere of hyper-reality, where the representation takes on a completely different 'life' and becomes valid in its own right and not just a subjective imitation or copy of what is perceived as the real, tangible thing.

However, it should be quickly said that this whole area is nothing new. Artists and story-tellers have indulged in subjective representations since people began talking. Of course, they have. That is how the Greek myths or Viking tales were handed down. The referent or original act has long been forgotten, to be replaced by countless subjective renderings and exaggerations. Every society uses the tools of its age to depict the world the way it wants to.

Film-makers and television serials are the current method of telling tales in our society - made to reflect the 'mood' of our society. And so, we watch war films, which glorify 'our' side and treat the enemy as evil, merciless swines, who have no place on our planet. The real 'truth' may be another story - but our movies have become the 'new truth'. Only time will tell if these current 'stories' stand the test of time and become the 'real' truth.

One of my favourite films is the Michael Caine epic, 'Zulu'. It told the story of a heroic defence of a small medical station, by a small number of British troops in the South African bush, in the 1870s.

The whole thrust of the film was to show how the courage and bravery of a few men can prevail over impossible odds (i.e. a Zulu 'impi' of several thousand warriors, sent to annihilate them). The film was applauded at the time as being an accurate representation of the real event, after which a record number of 11 Victoria Crosses were awarded. The film also 'starred' the South-Wales Borderers as the true heroes, with several colourful characters adding texture to the film (e.g. Henry Hook – the down-to-earth malingerer, who comes good in the end).

The fact that the South-Wales Borderers were not actually the company that took part in the real action or that the real Henry Hook was a quiet, Bible-fearing soldier, have no relevance anymore. The representation of the reality now has more 'truth' than the real thing, because this is the story that people have seen and bought into. The film has become actual history. In years to come, people will see Michael Caine and Stanley Baker as the true images of Bromhead and Chard (the 'real' officers in charge at Rorke's Drift) and will remember the soldiers singing 'Men of Harlech' as the Zulus attacked (despite the fact that 'Men of Harlech' had not been written when the battle actually took place!).

Incidentally (as an aside to the current discussion), it is also interesting to see how perceptions of this film have changed over time. Back in the 60s, Britain still saw itself as a major player in the world and films like Zulu only enhanced this feeling. Nowadays, the film is rarely shown, because it could be argued in the politically-correct society that we currently live in, that it has racist and even anti-feminist undertones. Heroic defence has become colonial carnage.

Moving on from Zulu… and taking all this to the bizarre extreme, a newspaper article recently highlighted the problem in Indian schools with their textbooks.

Here we have the referent/representation taking on a completely different life. So, what did this article (which, of course, is itself a subjective representation) claim? Well, for starters that David Bowie and Freddie Mercury were not only great musicians, but that they also invented desalination. Yes, that is correct - they solved the salty water problem in India! Once you have recovered from that revelation, we are told that Japan dropped a nuclear bomb on America, not the other way around! It becomes very clear, very quickly, that this textbook has been written by someone with a very vivid and creative imagination and not what we would consider 'factual' history.

The article ends by saying that the offending textbook has now been taken out of the school curriculum, but you have to wonder that a generation of Indian children are growing up still believing what they were initially taught… and then telling these 'stories' to their children. Even if there was just one person, who believed that it was Japan that perpetrated the ultimate nuclear attack, that should be enough for the 'story' to continue down through future generations in at least one small Indian village.

The 2019/20 Amazon television series 'Hunters' also sparked controversy in its portrayal of 'life' in the

German concentration camps of the Second World War. The problem here is whether such appalling atrocities, which are still fresh in the mind, should be the subject of fictionalised drama. By its nature, fiction like this is clearly not the 'truth', but a representation of what 'might have happened', given the historical records. The show was accused of 'Jewsploitation' for its fictional atrocities, specifically for 'inventing' a game of human chess. Kevan Pollack of the Holocaust Educational Trust said: "We have a responsibility to protect the truth particularly as we are moving away from living history - the survivors are few and frailer." At the crux of the argument was the producer's (David Weil) assertion that the show 'was inspired by true events', and that he never intended it to be a factual documentary. The counter argument is that such fiction will become 'fact' in years to come as people remember the show and not the history.

Heavens knows what future generations (say, in a thousand years' time), will think or believe of our era. You only have to look at the Greek myths to realise that stories get tangled, confused, exaggerated, added to and sensationalised, to create the required storytelling effect on an awed audience.

The writer, Jean Baudrillard, called these fanciful offshoots from the original – simulacra, a hyper-real variant of the real thing. And, in so doing, he saw simulacra as totally different 'entities' to the original referent. It had gone far beyond any representation. And so, in this 'world', Freddie Mercury did invent desalination and Japan did drop an atomic bomb on America.

The hyper-real world is capable of all stories at all times and all interpretations! It is a place which began as a copy of our real world and has developed, changed, and metamorphosed into something very different. It is a universe of strange possibilities, of multiple simulacra, which we have created to answer the needs of a population that is growing more and more tired of the 'real' thing. Those Indian children probably loved the idea of famous musicians lending a hand with their fresh water problem. Those stories will stick, no matter what subsequent teachers will say, because they are good stories!

And with the Internet, we can create more of our own stories and our own histories, quite easily. What is more, we can now enter these dream (or nightmare) worlds and actually live some sort of existence there, with VR (Virtual Reality) and all of that kind of thing. We can live in worlds where Japan did drop an atomic bomb on America. Video games are already out there telling these 'alternative' histories. So, in a very spurious way, what those teachers were teaching Indian children, was, in a sense, 'true'. After all, what is truth in this digital age?

It is a sobering thought that we are now living in an age where the simulacra have as much, if not more relevance and meaning than the referent (or original), which is probably another reason why Ash and I run all over Bromley trying to catch a MewTwo or a Rayquaza!

5. anything can happen in the next half hour!

Moving on a brisk canter – and we arrive at the staggering success of Bitcoins. I know that this is a somewhat startling jump from bombs, Freddie Mercury and Zulu, but it is another fine example of the representation argument. Honestly.

Initially meant as a global currency, it is now threatening to become more valuable than the US dollar. And don't forget that the US Dollar was itself a somewhat flimsy representation… initially. Gold was the standard by which wealth has always been always measured. Since the beginning. Centuries ago. The referent. The solid, tangible hunk of reality we can all look at and measure wealth with. That was the ultimate 'referent' of wealth. Why? Because it is really scarce, can easily be shaped into jewellery and probably because it looks pretty cool too.

Then along came the paper dollar. That took a lot of convincing as a valid substitute for the valuable yellow metal. It was President Nixon who declared that the dollar would no longer be 'dependant' on gold for validity, but would be valid in its own right. The representation suddenly was recognised as a referent in its own right.

And now, crypto-currency has come along with its representation of paper money. Here we have a currency, which does not exist, is not recognised by any governments or countries, does not have any tangible banks or even a visible currency. It exists totally in the world of virtual reality. And yet… it has become more powerful and valuable in just 10 years than all other currencies. People who bought Bitcoins in 2009 are now multi-billionaires in the 'real' world. Here we have a breathtaking example of the simulacra becoming a new referent in itself, with absolutely no relationship at all to what it started out representing. A Bitcoin is as far from a hunk of gold as a bicycle is from a Ferrari!

So, there you have it. We have moved in just a few pages from Matisse's pipe, via David Bowie, to Bitcoins. Now that is postmodernist thinking! Chaos, non-sequiturs and illogicality on every line!

Iron Man and black people in China

I recently saw a short 'meme' on YouTube, which showed someone dressed up as 'Iron Man' jump out in front of a little old woman somewhere in the middle of China. The old woman did not even bat an eyelid. She was not even surprised. But when the man took off his mask to reveal a black man as the prankster, she yelped in astonishment and jumped away.

Why? Because the unreal world is far more acceptable in her world. Chinese men running around in Iron Man suits must be pretty common place in her village, or at least, watching the many

Iron Man movies is. However, upon seeing a black man, she reacted with terror. He had far more impact than people dressed up as Iron Man.

Why? Well, in China, black people are generally only seen on television and action films, where guns, shooting and varieties of assorted violence are commonplace. They have become associated with crime and violence, but ironically, not in the same way as Iron Man. And so, she reacted accordingly. With fear and anxiety. In her eyes, black men were associated with 'bad' violence, while Iron Man was all right, because his was 'good' violence.

Maybe though, the best reason for her surprise was that Iron Men were commonplace in her village, whilst black people were extremely rare and therefore scared the old woman.

But you also have to address the reasons for her fear of a black man, in the first place. Her feelings and emotions of the real world have been preconditioned by the hyper-real world of television, where black people are seen as odd, dangerous and threatening!

Which leads us, quite naturally, to Donald Trump

...since he is always an outstanding example of something.

He is a billionaire businessman with multiple luxurious residences, an exotic lifestyle and all the power he can wield. And yet, he sells himself to the American people as being 'one of them'. He talks straight. He says things he should not. He has the frailties of the common man and he speaks a language they understand. He is a master of language manipulation and anti-marketing – or at least he could be. He could all also be just a rich man stumbling around firing his six-shooter in all directions with some bullets hitting their mark, while others miss horribly or hit innocent people. Your choice.

The irony is that Donald Trump is as far away from 'normal' people's lifestyles as is humanly possible. He is most definitely not one of them. But he talks the talk and walks the walk. He sounds like one of them, which is the most important thing.

Trump is a prime example of postmodern contradiction. He is a representation of something that never existed. Trump was never an ordinary, 'common' person with money and job worries. He has no underlying truth. He says he represents the person in the street, despite never being that person. He says he stands up for the silent majority in America – the person with limited hope, money and intelligence. And he communicates with these people by using simple, short sound-bites. And a vast proportion of the American people love this. Why?

Because it is the first time in living memory that a politician can be 'understood'. Trump avoids logical, long, dull, unintelligible arguments that traditional politicians use. Intelligence and reason are things of the past. They are mistrusted because no one understands them anymore. People glaze over when confronted with blurred, woolly, politically-correct responses in a complicated language which rarely actually answers the question.

Reality, logic, truth and wisdom are no longer important in the world today whether you are a Trump or a Trump hater. All wheel and deal in their own subjective interpretation of the truth.

Trump wields his soundbites in pithy contradiction, almost at whim. Take the 'wall'. At one stage, it was going to be built by 'Mexico', then it was going to be funded by massive taxes placed on Mexican goods coming into the US and finally, it was going to be paid for by legislation through the two houses in Washington. Trump has shifted his enemies from Mexico to taxes on cheap Mexican goods and finally to Democrats blocking his 'wall' legislation.

He fights a different enemy depending on his mood... and contradicts himself at every turn. He is a classic example of the man in the pub with loud views on anything that comes to mind. At first, the Mexican president was the devil-incarnate - then, he is shaking hands with him. Then it was refugee 'caravans', described as invading armies until people drowned in the Rio Grande. Finally, and predictably, it was the Democrats. If we view Trump as an 'intelligent' politician, then this might be a logical, artful progression with a presidential election looming on the horizon.

Trump is a marriage of vastly different doctrines and arguments, if you can call them that. Defending the common people, the planet, workers' rights and the US border in one breath... and then big business, the military, and large steel corporations, in the next. If anyone exemplifies the postmodern incredulity, it is him. His whole 'philosophy' is to keep everyone else permanently off-balance. And, if anyone comes along with a solid counter-argument, or attacks him in any dangerous or personal way, he can immediately step behind the shield of fake news. He uses his version of hyper-reality (fake news), representations and simulacra to confound his critics. And he succeeds… despite everything.

If we are to be kind, we could argue that he is just a businessman, who switches position and adapts arguments just to get the deal. Say anything – it does not mean you mean it! Just do the unpredictable and keep everyone guessing. That not only creates an air of excitement, worry, anxiety and incredulity, but also shows Trump to be a man who is capable of almost anything at any given moment.

OK… enough of the Donald, for now - I feel I have wandered from the point, so let's dive into a little more postmodernism on a more personal scale, without more ado. I feel a story coming on.

Be seeing you!

So, when did all this stuff first poke its irritating head above the parapets… for me?

Well, it was as long ago as 1964, even though I did not realise it then. Postmodernism is like that. It creeps up on you and surprises you when you are least expecting it.

As an 11-year-old boy, who loved stories of the stars, I had been entranced by Gerry Anderson's puppet extravaganza, *'Fireball XL5'*. I am showing my age here, I know, but needs must... Then came along *'Stingray'*. At first, I was not a fan – it was set in the oceans of the world. Boring. But it grew on me and... eventually, I was won over. Never in the history of puppetry has there been a more revolutionary and ground-breaking children's programme.

First, the whole premise of the show was world peace and saving the planet – not blowing up things or killing as many aliens as possible; second, the hero was involved in a love triangle with the commander's daughter, Atlanta and a mysterious mute girl, Marina; third, the commander of the good guys was disabled – moving around in a hover-chair; fourth, the mute girl had lived a life of constant abuse as a slave in the underwater realms of the Aquaphibians; fifth, the hero's partner and buddy (Phones) was as obsessive-compulsive as you could find in a puppet.

It broke the rules everywhere - disability, feminism, love-triangles, obsessive-compulsive issues, abuse, threesomes, emotional turmoil, to name but a few of the issues tackled. Even the episode titles were as 'zany' as possible – probably reflecting the 'grooviness' of the time. *'Titan Goes Pop'*, *'The Cool Cave Man'* and *'Pink Ice'* are three splendid examples. It was also the first programme to be transmitted in colour on UK television and, to top it all, the voice of Atlanta, was none other than Lois Maxwell, Miss Moneypenny in 14 James Bond films.

I could go on and on about Stingray – it was so far ahead of its time, it would probably have trouble getting aired on today's children's television without multiple warnings beforehand. It was 60s postmodernist genius, because it addressed so many issues, broke new ground, recognised no rules and did it all in a bizarre, fantastical, hyper-real way.

Enough of Stingray, but If you want more cutting-edge, early postmodernism on the screen at that time, then look no further than sour-faced Patrick McGoohan in 'The Prisoner'. Genius on so many levels and totally incomprehensible to all but a small, dedicated, nerd-fraternity, who still probably wear No. 6 badges and say 'Be seeing you', whenever they meet up.

The programme was as fragmented as it gets, set in an isolated village by the sea, somewhere in an unknown country. The buildings were a mish-mash of styles from British, Greek, Italian to East European. The viewer was kept permanently off balance. Cutting-edge technology was also installed throughout 'The Village' with electric front doors, small taxi beach-buggies, a Tannoy system informing residents of the latest news and a very scary security drone, shaped like a massive white balloon, which roared all the time and was called Rover.

It was also, of course, a prisoner trying to escape. Man against the establishment, man against a nightmarish big-brother future, No. 6 against No. 2, good against evil, logic against insanity and man against technology. It was about drugs, mind control, resilience, courage, madness and was as psychologically-complicated as any show made before or since. It used pastiche, parody, schizophrenia and humour to cutting effect, with some episodes branching off completely into other genres (e.g. the western episode, *'Living in Harmony'*). It did not respect time, plot construction or thriller convention. One second, the hero was playing cricket, the next, he was being interrogated or injected with hallucinogenics, or being elected as president of The Village. Genius or nonsense? Up to you. But postmodernist, jaw-dropping and rule-breaking, definitely.

Postmodernism all over the place

I should quickly say here and now (more to justify this increasingly-lengthy meander into the foothills of postmodernism) that I believe that you need a broad outline on all things postmodernist, before having a bash at postmodernist marketing. You need to know what is going on around you in all genres, spheres and areas to be able to wield anti-marketing effectively, or you will fail. Understanding a society's culture, beliefs, history and art etc. is fundamental to postmodernist or anti-marketing.

So, let's continue down this path a little more and look at another nice quotation, which should gently lead us into the sphere of marketing.

"Postmodernism is best understood not just as a style, but as a general orientation, as a way of apprehending and experiencing the world and our place, or placelessness, in it" (Gitlin, 1989).

It has been said that the digital age is 'post-everything' and that art, architecture, science, engineering, literature, music and marketing are all deeply affected by its influence.

And here is another conundrum to ponder on - postmodernism has a completely different meaning and set of values, depending on what genre or sphere you are poking around in. For example, in architecture, it could be the Sydney Opera House or pretty much any Frank Gehry edifice. Put simply, it is any building which breaks down the traditional barriers of space and form (i.e. not the standard, rectangular prism, on its end). My father used to say that postmodern architecture was any modern building that rooted you to the spot and made you say 'Wow' quite loudly.

In the film industry, you just have to watch the 1969 movie, *'Zabriskie Point'*. It examines the clash of the modern and the postmodern in very simple terms. Modernism has become staid, dull, blocky and very establishment. Postmodernism is seen as younger, more vital, freer and totally without rules. Breathtaking, yet amazing and menacing, at the same time.

Stanley Kubrick's *'2001: A Space Odyssey'* (1968) is another great example. It was a stark break with convention and the norm, covering three distinct, fragmented, time periods, containing no speech for the first 20 minutes, having that famous battle of man against the machine and having an ending which few understood; while being swept away by the majesty of the whole movie. And let's not forget the space ship sequence set to 'The Blue Danube' waltz. This is as postmodern as you could get on celluloid. High and low culture in the fractured hyper-reality of space.

Other pretty good examples are the movie, *'Blue Velvet'* and the TV series, *'Twin Peaks'*. Then there is the original *'Blade Runner'*, with its apocalyptic vision of a dystopian future, dominated by advertising, product placement and hyper-real realities, which have become indistinguishable from the 'real' thing. Boundaries between time periods have been torn down. The past is the present is the future. Images, dreams or nightmares, can be vividly depicted in ways never 'dreamt' of before. Violence is on a titanic scale and yet, because it is so hyper-real, we feel disconnected with the horror depicted. Nothing is hidden. Everything is exposed. Yet nothing is real because it is so fantastical and in another time and universe.

In literature, postmodernism relies heavily on fragmented plots, paradox, irony, black humour and a decentred universe. Beckett, Pynchon, Vonnegut, Heller and even James Joyce all come to mind. There is considerable magic realism evident as humans come to grips with an unforgiving and disparate universe.

Postmodern music is far harder to summarise, since there is no real 'movement' to concentrate on, no distinct 'markers'. You could argue that Philip Glass fits the bill, or Brian Eno, David Bowie and Pink Floyd. Certainly, The Beatles are in there too, of course, with their psychedelic ventures, as is the whole area of improvised jazz. For me, it was probably progressive rock and then punk, which highlighted postmodernism in its most brutal form.

Progressive rock broke from the 3-minute 'single' norm and gave the listener grandiose 25-minute swirling epics, which contained fragmented elements of classical, pop and rock music with incomprehensible lyrics. The themes covered everything from religion to history. Yes's *'Gates of Delirium'* is a fine example, being a lavish 25-minute rock opera of Tolstoy's War and Peace - a confused musical epic of chaos, fever and discordance.

Punk was the exact opposite – again breaking the norm. Low culture glorified in stark, brutal, overt attacks on the establishment, the upper class and royalty – very short tuneless, fragmented, angry songs, which were embraced by the rebellious young as a break with everything that had gone before. A savage attack on anything vaguely high culture and instantly accessible and understandable to the masses.

As for art, it is a little easier. Most movements have defining points, like Picasso's *'Les Demoiselles d'Avignon'* arguably heralding modernism, back in 1907. Postmodern art stretches across a very broad area and probably encompasses everything from Warhol to Banksy, with shades of Tracey Emin and Christo thrown in for good measure. Artists who have broken the barriers down in the last thirty years or so and are now viewed as either visionary pioneers, or as peddlers of the absurd.

Whatever you may think, they all have a place at the dinner table of postmodernism, because they were asking different questions and not adhering to any established and fundamental rules of modernism. Plus, crucially, they did something different, dangerous, risky and completely unique.

Why is all this important to the marketing person?

Well, if you have to ask that question, you should probably go back to page one of this handbook and start again, or give up and play Candy Crush instead...

So, there you have it. Unpredictable, different, odd, silly, thought-provoking, but always exciting and remarkable.

Tidying things up

Postmodernism is not a coherent or structured movement. It is also not a force for good (or bad) - it has many positive slants and just as many negative ones. And there have been many interpretations and explanations as to what it is – some instantly understandable and some deeply complicated and embedded in philosophical theory. The incredulity to meta-narratives is just scratching the end of the trunk of the elephant, which is still brooding quietly in the corner.

But you may still be wondering what pipes, Stingray, Number 6, Donald Trump, Pink Floyd and Banksy have got to do with marketing and anti-marketing. Well, to be totally honest, not much. But, in laying down the foundations of understanding what postmodernism could be, they are sort of valid, to some degree.

All of the examples above have shown that what we perceive as the real world, is not quite as easy to explain. Matisse's picture of the pipe may seem just a rather obvious lateral puzzle (when explained). And it can be argued that in some hyper-real sense that even Donald Trump is valid.

As for the relevance of all this to anti-marketing, all will be become relatively clear very soon, since postmodernism and its many contradictions, distortions and oddities have great relevance to everything that anti-marketing and postmodernist marketing stand for.

Everything in this shadow world relies on bizarre simulacra, strange representations and the ability to view Matisse's pipe in all sorts of new, fun and remarkable ways.

6. Adolf Hitler and bushbabies

Traditional marketing experts have always doggedly tried to ignore postmodernism's presence, or explain it away as just an interesting and quirky new 'fad', or a lively offshoot of traditional marketing methods, which are founded on the 'marketing mix' and those four Ps.

Right, let's get straight down to it - we have to start somewhere with this brief toe-dipping into the lake of postmodernist gloop... so let's give 'decentralisation' a brief kick around. Just a brief kick, mind. To give you an idea of the cunning way that postmodernism has infiltrated most things we do, nowadays.

It has been said that postmodernism 'decentralizes' the customer by putting him or her into separate, fragmented contexts in daily life. What on earth does this mean?

Put simply, the customer is no longer seen as just the end of the marketing process. 'Decentralisation' sees everything as just part of a much longer game, where the customer is involved in all areas of the pre-production, development and 'post-consumption' processes. He or she is not just the passive target of all marketing endeavours. The customer is viewed as being the 'controlling' factor in all the processes, actually becoming part of the marketing team and whole selling experience.

'In postmodernity, consumers seek different and local experience and they desire to belong to processes and experience immersion in thematic settings rather than merely encounter finished products and images. Therefore, marketing has to involve the consumer by considering him as a producer of experiences.' (Cova, 1996)

And that's decentering in a nut-shell. We will look at it in a little more detail in a later section. But first, a little more toe-dipping, let's introduce another interesting area – segmentation.

More stuff

The main problem was that in the past, marketing theories relied on the stability of markets and a nice ordered, easily segmented marketplace, which rested on solid socio-economic foundations with a clear 'class' structure, a certain intelligence, neat age segmentation and the sanctity of the family 'unit'.

Yes, we have now moved onto that tricky beast called 'segmentation'. It has been claimed that to segment a market successfully, the analyst has to be able to measure buying behaviour, product preference, usage and loyalty, along with demographics such as age, location, customer size etc.

But things have changed. And are still changing. Nowadays, there is much less of a class divide, politics are confused, loyalty is ephemeral, behaviour sporadic and the family unit is fragmenting, irretrievably. We live in an impatient, superficial age, where not just families have disintegrated, but individuals within families have also fragmented in so many different ways, all impatiently demanding a constantly-changing set of fragmented products. Even our fragmentation has fragmented and divided multiple times and in multiple ways.

We are left with what Stephen Brown calls *'immeasurable intangibles'*. What makes it worse is that the postmodernist believes that customers can no longer be clustered together with like-minded individuals. The 21st century consumer wants individuality and uniqueness. He or she wants to join one 'segment' and then switch to another at the drop of a hat and without any discernible reason.

It is no wonder that traditional marketing has struggled to adapt. Traditional marketing people will probably shrug all these anomalies off and claim that whatever happens, the 4 'Ps are still appropriate and that the marketing mix will save the day, since they are like Einstein's theories of relativity – solid, set in stone and upon which marketing reality is based. To challenge them would mean challenging everything that has been set down before. Rigid rules with no allowance for any… bending.

Conversely, postmodernism, with its acceptance of uncertainty, subversion, rootlessness and fragmentation, welcomes a certain 'bending'. It happily embraces innovation, achievement, exuberance and uniqueness, as well as allowing for stagnation, entropy and enfeeblement into its marketing mix.

It truly is a mixed bag of contradictions and is always on the *'brink of collapsing into confusion'* (*Stephen Brown, The Postmodern Condition, 1995*).

Before we get to grips with all the strange effects of postmodernist marketing and this thing called anti-marketing, let us take a small step sideways and tackle one important issue head on, which is fundamental to postmodernist and anti-marketing.

The customer is no longer important

Stephen Brown (*'Free Gift Inside', 2003*) said that *'disregarding the customer increases desire; denying everything increases determination; depriving the customer increases desperation; deferring drives customers to distraction; 'delving' inspires devotion and desisting causes disorientation.'*

Clearly, Professor Brown was having his own 'd' day when he put this list together. He does, however highlight the fact that the customer is no longer king (or queen) anymore. The processes of marketing, according to Brown, should not depend on being 'nice' all the time to the customer. Here we have another postmodern contradiction. Traditional marketing set the customer on a pedestal and did everything he or she desired. The customer ruled. He or she demanded something and the marketing person would hastily provide.

Brown dethroned the customer completely. The 'd's are a total reversal of traditional marketing tactics and puts marketeers on the throne instead. After all, marketing people are the experts, not the customer. They know what is best for us all. Honestly.

However, since Brown wrote this in 2003, things have radically changed and it could now be argued that everything has become much more muddled, if that is possible. Put simply, the marketeer is no longer king or queen – a brief reign indeed.

Why? Because we are all kings or queens now. The whole nine yards – everyone, because we are all customers, sellers, buyers and marketeers. All mixed up together. Those 'd's are certainly still valid, but apply to us all, marketeer, seller and customer alike. We 'disregard' and 'deny' our customers as they do to us, filling us with 'determination' and 'desire'. We are all 'deprived', 'disorientated' and… 'desperate', pretty-much all of the time. It is a mish-mash of emotions as we do our best to be… different (I'm feeling rather smug that this is a 'd' that Stephen Brown did not use).

Marketing has moved from neon-lit offices, PowerPoint presentations and 30-page campaign plans to everyone's back bedroom. We can all do our own thing and make our own mistakes whenever we want, while depriving or enthusing our own customers, who, in turn, deprive and enthuse us. We are all nicely part of the whole decentred process.

This 'un-professionalizing' of marketing makes every one of us a heady mix of marketing guru, sales expert and bungling amateur. We have truly slipped into postmodern chaos where rules apply to all and yet to none of us. Actually, if we are to be scrupulously honest, where there are no rules at all.

Enter... the Vlogger

Let's take a small step back and… enter the room occupied by postmodernist marketing chaos. This is just a brief example of how it has all gone to hell-in-a-handcart and why serious marketing theorists should now just give up completely and start writing about something else. It is a place where the customer really is no longer important, a place where we 'pull' or 'attract' the customer like a moth to a firework. That is one view, anyway.

The successful marketing person of today is not the person with the experience, qualifications, intelligence, belief or cunning and with amazing powers of persuasion or indeed, anti-persuasion. It is quite simply the person who has… followers.

Yes… followers. Acolytes. The masses. Crowds. People. Sheep (and I mean that in a nice way – I like sheep).

The use of YouTube and 'vlogs' (video logs) highlights this aspect of the 'un-professionalising' of marketing. Random people, who happen to have achieved fame via a bizarre set of vastly different routes, are now our marketing leaders. And it is not because they have a magical touch when it comes to marketing, or have created a new, unstoppable way of attracting potential customers. What rules the day is nothing more than the number of 'viewers' or 'followers' that they may have at any given time. It is the number of people who log on to watch them do silly things. It is as daft as that.

If the vlogger starts getting millions of people watching his or her vlogs, then big businesses sit up and start taking notice. It does not really matter if the 'chat' is inane, superficial and of no real importance – what matters is follower number. Nothing else.

You can be talking about fashion in London; giving tips about how to combat dragons in the gaming world; dancing to Brazilian pop songs; walking the streets playing *Pokémon Go*, giving demonstrations of Korean cooking; discussing the Kardashians hairstyles or getting angry about the Royal Family… if you are entertaining, funny and have buckets of charisma, then you are halfway there. It is like having your own show on the Internet and, if the thing goes viral and your viewer numbers go through the metaphorical roof, then you really can start thinking about that red Ferrari. You have become a one-person marketing machine without even trying.

Take the online site 'Twitch'. This involves online gamers worldwide. It is not a site which tries to sell games or even to encourage players to play on the site. It is simply there for 'watchers' or game 'voyeurs'.

Sure, gaming experts log in and play their own game. We are not interested in them. They are just part of the fabric of the site. It is the not so proficient gamer that we are interested in. These gamers (in their millions) just log in and… watch.

So, if you want a nice easy afternoon in "World of Warcraft' or "Call of Duty' without the stress and tension of being wiped out every five minutes, then settle back and watch a Chinese guy in Shanghai negotiate the perils for you. You can even see the player him or herself, in the corner of your screen, tapping away on his or her headphones and muttering the 'f' word every thirty seconds. Entertainment indeed! Across the top of the gaming screen are advertisers keen to get exposure to the Chinese guy's followers. The player may even have an avatar name which reflects a brand, which is paying him or her for exposure – or he or she may be wearing a t-shirt covered in paid branding, like a Formula 1 driver. And the number of people watching – this varies from a few hundred to many millions. Marketing gold dust! Being paid to march around fantasy land, swearing at your screen and looking… cool.

The site offers an almost movie-like atmosphere, which has tension, plot and real-time action. Here we have the new type of marketing superstar – someone who simply exists in the half-world of reality/hyper-reality and inane witter. These people are not experts or particularly clever – they are simply 'normal' people doing what they are good at, while dropping in the odd comment about Pepsi or Papa John's, as they wipe out German stormtroopers or undead beastmen from the planet Zog!

And yet, people are fascinated, drawn in and hypnotized in much the same way that millions are fascinated by not very intelligent people talking about nothing of value or interest in the many reality shows on television. It is just the fact that these people have acquired 'celebrity-status' by doing something different or well, that gives them their importance to society... and marketing.

And masses of followers who log in every day to watch their antics.

But there is a downside (there always is)

Amateurishness is always a great crowd-puller, because it is watching ourselves mess up in front of millions. It is both appalling, terrible and sometimes humorous, especially if the vlogger has not done his or her homework and inadvertently says something that is controversial. You can be playing a game or chatting away on your Vlog about bushbabies in Africa. And then, it happens. An unplanned Donald Trump moment... and you 'blurt' out something that happens to drift across your tired, untrained mind.

Why you associate Adolf Hitler with bushbabies, or mention monkeys inappropriately, you will never know. It just happens. Initial horror follows and instant deletion... but the damage has been done and you are on the front pages. Much condemnation. Even hatred. The 'twittersphere' goes into meltdown as the outrage ripples out to the four corners of the globe. This, of course, creates an even bigger 'buzz' to your reputation. Good news is great, but bad news can be even better. And follower numbers quadruple overnight. You might be bad, but you now are worth four times as much as before to the marketing people in the shadows.

This is the age of the amateur. And so, mistakes happen. But, so what? A mess today will be forgotten tomorrow, except that your follower number will increase dramatically. And anyway, a controversial and error-strewn player will gain a certain degree of 'anti-foundationalist' kudos, which should attract another swathe of followers, keen to have a laugh at a cruel world.

Another fly in the ointment

Being an expert dragon slayer with a humorous personality is one way of gaining fame and fortune. For the rest of us trying to make a fast buck in the 21st century, we have to think of other ways.

We need to discover our own paths of going 'viral'. We are all looking for that amazing moment. This is, as Malcom Gladwell ('*The Tipping Point*, 2000) says: '*when ideas trends, social behaviour cross a threshold – tip - and spread like wildfire.*'

Never mind £250 from '*You've been Framed*', - we are looking for that thing that will go around the world in a few seconds. The wildfire moment that will make our name a household word. This is our dream. We want to poke our heads up above the crowd and be noticed.

And this is another aspect of postmodernism. It is the struggle for individuality within an increasingly restrictive universe. It is a shout to prove that the individual matters and that each person really is totally unique and has something to say. Admittedly, you could argue that this has always been the case…

since time immemorial. The difference now is that the Internet has given us all a megaphone to help us tell our own story.

The vlogger is a great example of the chaos in marketing at the moment, where the best moments are unplanned and where experts have no place, except to be in the background, counting the money. The vlogger can be illiterate, uniformed and ignorant, but pointed in the right direction and he or she can make almost any product sell like hot cakes.

What is certain is that marketing today has become a very unstable process, which relies on factors, which have nothing to do with logic, reason or good planning, but rests on a constantly-moving bed of human unpredictability.

And what has all this got to do with sales and marketing?

Well, everything and nothing. Everything, because to be successful today in the digital world, the marketing person has to understand people better. Everything because suddenly the customer is vitally important to the whole marketing process.

And… it is nothing, because the Internet is just a cynical reflection of the sad age that we are living in. An age where a woman who talks about her hair interminably and with a million followers, is the new market leader. An age where a man can spend ten minutes every day shouting obscenities on YouTube and has ten thousand giggling followers. An age where a man who drinks a gallon of cola in twenty seconds has over a hundred thousand followers and can attract the likes of Coca Cola and Pepsi to pay him the really big bucks to drop advertisements into his mess. An age where a Peruvian in Lima can command a platoon of German stormtroopers in WW2 and wreak havoc with the British and Americans all day long and be watched by millions globally, while he carries out his killing spree.

So, yes, the customer is no longer important in the process, simply because the customer is the process. All marketing people have to do, is take strategic advantage of the daftness all about us and grab hold of the coat-tails of the successful, 'viral', vlogging, error-strewn amateur.

Of course, it is not that simple, but I reckon I am pretty close to the mark.

SECTION THREE:

practical anti-marketing

7. what about anti-marketing?

It has been argued that anti-marketing is the radical arm of postmodernist marketing - the fundamentalist bit, the area inhabited by the extremists - the lunatic fringe - those people who use shock and horror to get attention. OK, maybe that is a little extreme, but it could be seen as the slightly more controversial area.

Others claim that anti-marketing is the next step in the evolutionary chain of marketing, a sort of super-improved type of 'pull marketing'.

More have said it is akin to postmodernist 'selling', being the practical application of postmodernist marketing theory - and could be labelled 'anti-selling', rather than anti-marketing, since it could be seen as the process of taking postmodernist theories to the market-place and testing them out.

Still more consider anti-marketing as an umbrella term for such areas as reverse-psychology marketing, principled selling, minimalist marketing etc. - the quirkier areas of postmodernist marketing.

Some see it as the place for green or ethical issues (i.e. marketing 'with a conscience'), where profits are not as important as saving the polar bear.

There are some who see anti-marketing simply as the bit that defies categorization, the area of marketing practice that should never work, but does… like 'Marmite' attacking its own product, or 'Go Compare' using an opera singer in a taxi to sell their comparison site. It is the area that defies logic and relies on an unpredictable public for success.

A few see anti-marketing as the bit that concentrates on disillusionment, uncertainty, scepticism and doubt in the market place.

Anti-Marketing could be viewed as defying conventional marketing theory, preferring to make fun of traditional advertising/marketing techniques, while attempting to 'connect' with potential customers by sharing the joke, the pain and the self-inflicted wounds with them.

It could be seen as a positive force, whereby the seller/advertiser/marketeer deliberately lampoons his/her own brand, or it could be used as a very negative force, where disaffected people/competitors deliberately attack another brand by guile, rather than outright venom. This is the beauty of anti-marketing – it resists the temptation to be a blunt instrument and is instead a delicate rapier which targets the weakest spot.

Take the luxury clothing manufacturer, Abercrombie & Fitch. When they rather contentiously decided to focus their marketing on what they described as the *'young, thin and the popular'*, it naturally raised the hackles of more than a few people. However, rather than condemn such a policy in the standard manner, the Californian writer, Greg Karber, decided to adopt a distinctly anti-marketing approach. He went out and bought as much old and second-hand Abercrombie clothing as he could and then distributed it to the poor and homeless who lived on the streets. This sparked a lot of anti-publicity which highlighted the Abercrombie & Fitch marketing policy, while underlining the plight of the homeless, who were not in any way, 'young, thin and popular' and yet were wandering the streets decked out in Abercrombie & Fitch clothing. The campaign creaked to a halt extremely quickly.

Anti-marketing could be seen as a way of weakening an existing brand, making it seem both ridiculous and, in the worst cases… 'the bad guy'. And all achieved by not doing anything overtly vindictive (and suable). It is the rapier attack, rather than the blunt instrument.

In the world of anti-marketing nothing is sacred. Black can be white and white, black, depending on how you perceive things. And brands can be built upon this (e.g. our old friends, Marmite and Guinness) or can be broken, as in the Abercrombie & Fitch example above.

Anyway, let's have a look at a few practical examples of what could be viewed as good, solid anti-marketing.

Ryanair, Aldi, Lidl and Argos

Anti-marketing is used very successfully with these four massive and very successful enterprises.

Ryanair gained a sizeable foothold in the short-haul, airline market, by freely admitting that service, comfort, leg-room, check-in procedures and minimal free baggage facilities were not of prime concern. Their marketing policy relied on lots of 'nots' to sell seats. Basically, you were not buying a memorable experience. Or a comfortable seat. Or food. You were simply buying a ticket to get from A to B, as cheaply as possible.

Aldi and Lidl sold their products on the premise that choice was sporadic, unpredictable, uncluttered and cheap. No one knew what would be in the store almost on a daily basis, not even the staff. But whatever came in, it would be incredibly good value.

All three companies sold on price. Nothing else. Marketing fripperies were stripped down to the bone. In Aldi and Lidl, produce was even left in their delivery cardboard boxes and, up to recently, bags were not provided to take your stuff away in.

As for Argos, more on them in a bit.

Ryanair, Aldi and Lidl sold themselves despite, not because of the customer. They decide what to sell, when to sell it and in what quantities.

In Ryanair's case, they just said that you would get to your destination without a delay and that your ticket would be ridiculously cheap. It was more like a bus. After all, you would not expect a three-course meal and a blanket on the 208 to Orpington. Ryanair made air travel almost mundane. Just another form of transport. Not like the bigger carriers, which sold their seats as an experience, a way of life and even a luxurious 5-star event. Ryanair sold the customer a seat and that was about it. If you wanted extras then fine… but you would have to pay for the privilege.

Aldi and Lidl offered all the basic products needed by the average household, plus a central aisle of 'surprise' goodies, which changed almost all the time. So, one day, you could buy a toolkit for the car and the next, a haunch of Spanish 'jambon', on a wooden display unit. Ironically, people actually quite liked this. It made them feel exclusive when they had bought something different and unexpected. The surprise element generated excitement and encouraged customers to visit the store every day, just to see what was on the central 'surprise' aisle. It might have been nothing special – but it might also have been something you had always wanted. And it was cheap.

Letting the customer do the work and providing minimum information, service and even choice seems to be what the modern customer appreciates. It is certainly not traditional marketing, where the customer is king.

The story of Aldi is a strange one, in many ways. Its origins were in Germany, where the customer is a completely different creature. There, it is fine to stack products in unattractive columns and have zero customer experience – as long as the prices are as low as possible. Germans are happy with that.

So, when Aldi moved to the UK, the big supermarkets did not consider them as serious competition, being aimed at the 'lower' end of the market. Waitrose, Tesco's and Sainsbury's continued as before, in contented union.

But, with the 2008 global financial and economic meltdown, suddenly people were counting their pennies and looking for cheaper, weekly grocery bills. Suddenly, Aldi (and Lidl) became popular. And it was not just the 'low' end of the market anymore, but the affluent middle-classes started doing their weekly shop there too. So, store numbers, sales and profits increased, mostly at the expense of Waitrose, Tesco's, Sainsbury's and even Morrisons.

It was then that the big supermarkets sat up and took notice. They did not like a foreign competitor muscling in on their 'monopoly'. So, they put the 'squeeze' on Aldi's suppliers, threatening to drop their business with them if they did not cease supplying Aldi.

At first, this looked like the end of Aldi. Until the German company thought very laterally and started producing its own goods with slightly different brand names and logos. It certainly trod the copyright tightrope when such products at Norpak, Magnum and Titan hit the shelves in packaging which looked extremely similar to Lurpak, Fairy and Mars. Now, as we know, customers are a suspicious bunch, and initially the idea of buying what looked like fake washing up liquid or an inferior Mars bar did not appeal. But, once tried and the customer was hooked. Virtually the same as the original and much cheaper.

The main thrust of the Aldi 'appeal' was cheapness and… speed. There were very few queues at checkouts, because of the incredible speed that cashiers checked products through their tills. This was achieved by having bar codes in more than one place on the product packaging… and much bigger. Customers were also encouraged to throw all their stuff back in their trolleys and then trundle to a special area at the exit of the store, where they could bag everything up slowly and at their own pace. So, no bottle-necks at the tills.

Then, Aldi produced its first television commercial, featuring a grandmother figure saying how much her husband loved tea. The beauty of the commercial was that the woman compliments the competitor on display (PG Tips), while giving Aldi's own brand (Red Label) similar air-play. The only (unsaid) difference was the price caption beneath each product, which showed how much cheaper the Aldi version was. And the final touch – the grandmother figure says that she herself disliked tea, preferring gin. Anti-marketing with panache.

This was the first shot across the bow of those claiming that Aldi products were in all ways inferior. It was designed to prove to a sceptical public that Aldi food and household products were in no way worse than the brands.

This was further enhanced by blindfold street tastings in crowded town centres; help from a highly-publicized McCann-Erickson survey and by television programmes examining the 'Aldi phenomena' (Channel 5 did a whole one hour documentary on

Aldi, which only just fell short of being the longest advertisement ever for supermarket).

Aldi then subtly rebranded the company to make it seem more like a traditional British one. Gone were all the German references, to be replaced by Union flags along with straplines proclaiming the Britishness of all the products on show. Aldi even sponsored the GB athletics team in general and the triathletes, the Brownlee brothers, in particular.

Aldi has now progressed up the supermarket food chain to replace Waitrose and the Co-Op, lying now just behind Sainsbury's and Tesco's in customer footfall and annual turnover. It truly has been a staggeringly quick incursion into such a tightly-controlled market.

What makes it even stranger is that Aldi is the only supermarket to have resisted the temptation for online ordering and speedy delivery to the customer's own front door. Why? Because to enter into that market would require many more storage depots and warehouses, as well as creating a huge and expensive delivery operation. All this would affect store prices – something that Aldi sees as the central core to their success and never to be compromised.

The ultimate compliment to Aldi is that Tesco's have created its own cheaper variant – JACK'S. This was designed to combat Aldi, but with the massive supermarket behind it. Only time will tell if this affects the Aldi success story.

Finally, let's look at Argos. No discussion on anti-marketing would be complete without talking about this High Street retailer. It epitomises everything that anti-marketing stands for.

I saw Sean Lock (a British 'stand-up' comedian) do a brilliant little skit on this exact topic. He imagined standing before the Dragons on the programme, *'Dragon's Den'*, and pitching the Argos idea.

The essence of the pitch was:

- Here we have a new type of shop, which is empty. It doesn't let the customer see any of the products, but just gives them a massive catalogue and a small, betting-shop pencil and order form. You have to flick through the catalogue, make your choice and then write down a long, complicated code number on the form. After that, you join a queue to a check-out and pay for your product. Then you join another queue at what looks like the back of a warehouse (because that is exactly what it is) to collect your product. Finally, a Tannoy announces your code and your stuff is slid over a counter still in its cardboard delivery box…".

It was at this point that the audience all laughed ruefully. And yet… the concept works. Against all logic and sense, it works. And has made millions for the owners of Argos. It is shopping experience pared down to absolute zero. Argos is the Ryanair of the High Street. No frills, no fancy lighting or smiling shop assistants. Just the product in a cardboard box at a price which reflects this lack of packaging or service.

The Dragons would most certainly have given such a pitch very short shrift and quickly moved onto their next victim.

We might be living in an age where customer experience means more now than ever before, but there are elements of anti-marketing which cut right across the grain of logic and contradict the whole sorry, chaotic mess.

So, there you have it - anti-marketing can be described as doing it all the wrong way… and somehow getting results.

It could be seen as the practical application of postmodernist marketing, or it might possibly be the fundamentalist extreme of it all. It could also be a nice umbrella definition for the sillier elements of modern marketing and sales, which work despite everything. And finally, it could just be a complete contradiction to everything I have said previously!

8. the English language industry

(this can easily be skipped over)

Take the English language industry

Why?

Because this is my own point of reference, having worked in and around it for about 35 years and because it is a rich source of all things modernist, traditional, controversial, postmodernist and extremely contradictory.

It has been estimated that this industry (yes, it really is an industry) creates a revenue of just over a billion pounds every year in the UK alone, if you throw everything in. I mean everything, not just the money rolling in for language course tuition fees. Stuff like host families, student residences, the bus companies that do all the excursions, the entrance fees to all the tourist attractions all over the UK and even the small shops around schools up and down the country that sell chocolates to cigarettes to students.

So, what are we talking about here? And how can our language be a product? OK, let's have a brief look at what it is. Brief because, as I keep saying, it is not that important in the grand scheme of things.

English is a language, which many people around the world want or need to learn, for a variety of reasons. The two most popular are: further education and jobs, of course. Many companies worldwide make English mandatory for their employees – from China to Colombia and Saudi Arabia to Russia. English speaking people really do not know how lucky they are. It is the language of the internet, computers, diplomacy and is used as the lingua franca in virtually all international meetings around the globe. It has become a vital commodity.

This is where schools, colleges and universities come in (and I am primarily talking about the UK here). I will not speak too much about the government institutions like universities and colleges either, since they are mostly public-funded and have a very different set of rules to the private sector. They can afford to be choosy when selecting their students and can charge enormous sums of money for a piece of paper with the letters BA or MA on the top. They can also concentrate on being academically-orientated. That may sound slightly silly, but it is an important difference, as you will see.

So, here we are. Private language schools. The front line in the war on English. In the academic trenches, up to their eyes in grammatical, communicative, humanist mud, without any real idea what to do next, except ring a class bell every 50 minutes and go over the top.

Private language schools have been around for over half a century now. And the tools of their trade – English courses. Standard, simple language courses -

loosely labelled: 'General English'. These are available to anyone with a desire to learn and come at any level, any time and for as long as the student wants.

And cobbled to this are all sorts of other courses, like examination courses for those needing a certificate badly, English for business - for executives with bottomless funds; teacher-training and junior programmes for the little ones. All are welcome. Private language schools offer a service to students needing an English course at all times of the year, which will not cost an arm and a leg.

Moreover, it should be quickly added that virtually all schools out there now are pretty good. They have to be or face instant closure and a centre page spread in the Sunday papers… plus large fines. The industry is regularly inspected, ransacked and regulated by a vigorous band of government inspectors.

You see, successive governments hate the private language school industry. It is viewed by them as a rather too convenient backdoor into the country for people who need visas extremely quickly. This might have been true in the past, but nowadays, even to breathe impropriety will bring the wrath of the men in peaked caps down onto you. It is mostly all above board today and offering a service which the short-term student actually prefers.

The marketing and sales teams

And it is into this heady mix that sales and marketing teams are dropped. Traditionally, this is not a marriage made in heaven. Academia and business are not very good bed fellows. Teachers, by their very nature, do not like sales people (and vice versa). It goes against the grain of everything that they have ever stood for. For them, money is a grubby necessity of life. As for sales people, money is the prime motivator and the reason to get up in the morning. It is chalk and cheese. Black and white. Heaven and Hell.

Teachers want to be able to give students a worthwhile experience and to improve their language levels and skills. Sales and marketing people, on the other hand, want the exact opposite – ideally, students should be slow learners, who have to extend their courses and… pay for the privilege.

Teachers work every day in high stress situations, facing banks of frowning students all trying to get to grips with the differences between: 'I ate dinner' and 'I have eaten my dinner.'

Sales and marketing people could not care less about the dining habits of students. 'Ate' and 'have eaten' mean the same thing – it is all food slipping down. Who cares about the difference? In fact, sales and marketing people would be hard pressed to know the difference, anyway!

It makes for an interesting clash of cultures. The language teaching industry could be seen as the archetypal anti-marketing business. It is an industry which exists not because of its goals, but in spite of them.

And the cherry on the cake

The major irony of the industry is that the sales people do not actually sell English courses to those people who need or want it. You would have thought that sales teams would be out scouring the world for students to come to their schools. But this is not the case. Far from it.

This is where 'language travel agents' enter the fray.

Language travel agents are a mixed bag of beasts, who generally have bright, snazzy offices in the downtown districts of busy university cities all over the world, from Bogota to Berlin and Caracas to Kuala Lumpur. It is their job to entice students with a dream, to learn a language like English, French, Spanish etc. in far flung corners of the English/French/Spanish-speaking world.

In Japan, the language travel agents are usually studious women with large glasses and a deep knowledge of how much better your competitors are. In Korea, it is middle-aged men in suits with desperate expressions on their faces. In China, it is men with bad haircuts and women who frown a lot. In Russia, it is women with power lipstick and soprano voices. In Germany, it is thin men with impressive desks. You get the picture? A mixed bag.

This is where the language school sales and marketing person goes with his or her bag of tricks and persuasive arguments. To get the big agent on board their ship is the prime aim of the sales people from a language school. Persuade them to sell your courses and then… sit back and watch the enrolments roll in.

Sure, sometimes sales teams attend public fairs and get a glimpse of the unfinished article (like the one in the story at the very start of this handbook), but these are few and far between. The bread and butter of the work is to get the language travel agent to do the serious heavy-lifting for them.

And this is where a whole new area of problems start popping up all over the place.

Language travel agents are:

1. **Rarely interested in the product (i.e. the English courses),** because they know next to nothing about it. Strangely enough, the English school sales person is similarly afflicted. It must be one of the very few industries where this happens – and yet business is still conducted happily and successfully - a case of the blind leading the blind in contented union. On neither side of the table is there much academic expertise on display

2. **Rarely interested in the price.** In fact, the cheaper you go, the less chance you get of selling your wares! Language travel agents operate on a commission basis and selling cheap courses is simply not worth the bother (i.e. commissions on cheap courses are very low), compared to the effort exerted in getting the booking. Plus… in today's society, students shy away from the cheap stuff anyway – because cheap implies inferior quality. Price is also a very fluid

commodity, what with currency fluctuations. It has ceased to be a deciding factor

3. **Rarely interested in the quality.** Language travel agents really have very little knowledge of what constitutes a 'quality' English course. They are business people, not academics. And anyway, it is all so subjective. Every school claims to be on 'top of the pile' because there are so many different ways of assessing quality. Most schools have a certificate from somewhere, a Star Award, or masses of points of excellence. They also all claim to have fantastic accommodation, superb facilities and a toilet on every floor. So – who to believe when every school says the same?

4. **Rarely interested in the 'packaging' or marketing material.** Why? Because most schools now have fancy websites (many are created and maintained by the similar web-design companies), which all look the same and claim the same USPs. They mean very little in the grand scheme of things

5. **Rarely solely interested in commission**. This may sound ridiculous, but your average 'good' agent will simply lay down the law that they require 30%, 40% or even 50% commission, before you even get to talk to them. It has ceased to be a point of interest, or part of any negotiation. It is just the basic ground rule to get you through the agent's door

So, if you are a traditional marketing and sales person, you have a problem. A big problem. 3 of the 4 Ps are gurgling down the drain, immediately.

What about location? To say that you have a great school in Cambridge, Oxford or London must count for something. Well, that is the final irony. It does not. Actually, in many cases it goes against the sales person in a meeting in the backstreets of Lima or Taipei.

For starters, most language travel agents worth their salt will already have a brochure full of the most popular cities in the world… and will simply not want anymore.

To be selling courses in Totnes in Devon, or Bury St. Edmunds in the east of England will certainly give you an angle on the uniqueness scale but, quite frankly, language agents have seen and heard it all before and are bored and disinterested in schools hailing from anywhere. It is hard enough nowadays to sell what they already have.

It is against this rather uncompromising backdrop that the English language sales person has to work his or her magic. It is an unenviable battle where money, quality, commission or location have as much worth as a bag of chips.

9. the maverick element

(some face-to-face, very practical stuff)

This is where anti-marketing is in its element

What can a sales and marketing person do, which is different, remarkable and rememberable?

Well, this is the bit that cannot really be quantified or taught, but it is the bit that truly distinguishes. Separates. Divides. The vital element in the selling process, when all the cobbled-together theories of chaotic, disordered, illogical postmodernism somehow are moulded into a struggling mass for the sales person tramping the street.

So, what is it?

Answer: The human element

This may seem slightly absurd. Actually, it sounds very absurd.

Surely, if you have a good product and a reasonable price in a great location with unbeatable commissions with the odd seasonal discount thrown in, then this should carry the day? And if not, the salesman can use all Brown's 'd's along with an assortment of principles, honesty and smiling eco-friendliness.

The human element has never been truly appreciated or quantified in selling and yet, it is arguably, still the crucial element. It is certainly recognised as a force in the selling process, but usually as an adjunct to the standard, traditional sales process. It is relatively easy to list the qualities needed to perform in a 'human' way. And there are many articles and books out there offering this advice.

Usually, these lists (modern and postmodern) involve a lot of building – relationships, trust, credibility, understanding, empathy... the list goes on and on. Then there is the 'personalisation' of 'your brand's story' and the offering of flexible and individualised solutions. And we must not forget personal integrity, honesty and even ethics. They all get thrown into the human-element-mix. One article I read recently was entitled: 'Connect with your customers on a deeper level' by 'showing your personality' and 'always being accessible'.

The main problem with these extremely praiseworthy pieces of advice is that hardly anyone has any ideas how to put them into practice. Again, it is left to the innate ability of the sales person somehow to be all of the above. And clearly in this digital age, virtually none are remotely possible.

Let's start with the Internet. It is a machine which extracts the humanity out of transactions. And ironically, the customer generally likes this, because of the instant nature of the beast and the incredible, inhuman speed. We have swapped the human element for the instant. Being nice and friendly do not really matter anymore. It is just the price and the discount that does.

But, strangely enough, when most people are asked, they claim that they prefer human interaction when it comes to customer service. Another contradiction. We all like to be treated as individuals and yet want to buy our stuff without talking to anyone. Ideally, we would like all businesses to employ millions of customer service advisors, who are instantly available whenever we ring up about a problem, day or night. We want our multiple-choice, drop-throughs and chatbots to be real people. Real people who are as good, efficient and speedy. Pie in the sky, I know.

The customer does not know what he or she wants anymore. The postmodernist marketeer recognises this. He or she knows that businesses have to rely on computers and a degree of 'inhumanization' to get the work done. We are not living in the 19th century anymore. And yet, there still has to be a human element in there. Not just a slither either – more like a spine running through the entire process.

The customer experience is changing.

Remember the story at the start of this handbook? The one about Seth Godin and his dust covers. The human element is everywhere in his emailed vlog. He uses the new technology to spread his 'quirky' personality far and wide. This is not just a book launch with glossy pictures and the odd quote. No, this is postmodern humanity manipulating modernist inhumanity in a very clever way.

Godin has masses of something which I can only describe as 'endearment'. How can you not like a cheeky chappie with his *'cause a ruckus'* and *'be remarkable'* strap-lines? He is the embodiment of the new type of sales and marketing person. He is not attractive (sorry, Seth) or has particularly winning arguments, but… he has something else. For want of a better word – charisma, quirkiness, endearment. He is also clearly not a sales person. He sits in a cluttered office, looking nervous and painfully aware of the camera. But… remember Kaa from the cartoon version of The Jungle Book. He has that sort of thing. And it is hard not like him.

There is one other factor which is necessary if you want the perfect anti-marketing mix. It is something which traditionalists would quickly back away from and reject out of hand. It is the anti-ability of being wrong. And actually, accepting this as a positive thing.

Now, I am not saying that a sales person should be deliberately wrong all the time – that would defeat the whole point. It is merely an acceptance of errors in the selling process as just human fallibility, showing the customer that the salesperson is really just another human being.

And oddly, the customer actually prefers the quirky, flawed sales person. We are back to customers selling to customers again, where not being the expert with all the answers, somehow underlines the honesty / trust factors.

So, perhaps the time is right in today's marketplace for the shortish, overweight, balding, nervous, badly-dressed, friendly and 'nice' individual (i.e. me), who makes mistakes, stutters a bit, loses concentration and even gets prices wrong. People are ready to believe this person far more, because they sound fallible. Vulnerable. And most of all, this type of sales person is clearly one of their own.

Throw in the fact that these flawed sales people genuinely want to give the customer a good deal and will happily keep in touch afterwards with lots of after-sales service and you have the successful 21st century anti-sales person!

Of course, just looking like a loser (or just a normal, person-in-the-street) will not carry the sales person over the line all the time. But it is a good start.

Other postmodern characteristics are needed. 'Anti-theory' needs to be converted into 'anti-action'. The fault-ridden sales person needs to tap into the dark matter of 'anti-marketing' and wield its power... without appearing to do so and in a non-threatening, unaggressive way.

So, instead of just indulging in rather bland lists – here is some actual, practical advice to the budding anti-marketeer, armed with a bag of tricks, a winning smile, a stained suit (or dress) and a dream...

Step ONE – wear a red nose and sing 'Oklahoma'

I once attended a sales seminar in London where the speaker (a rather fat man with perspiration problems and a permanent sniff) said that a sales person would be far more successful today, if he or she entered a meeting where a presentation was required, wearing a clown's red nose, no trousers and jumping onto the nearest table singing 'Oklahoma!'. Suicidal tactics, maybe, but there would be no doubt that you would be remembered forever.

This was the thrust of the session – to be remembered. And everything, according to this inspirational speaker, should be sacrificed to this end. Certainly, in the rarefied atmosphere of selling courses in the English language industry, you need to find something that will stay in the mind of the agent, who has heard it all before and just wants to go home.

So, how can we manage this? How can we be remembered?

Step TWO – throw up on your client

Several years ago, I was in Korea doing a presentation at the biggest agency in Seoul. I went with a colleague, who I will call Oli. This is not necessarily his real name. Halfway through a pretty impressive presentation, which we did like a 'Morecambe and Wise' sketch, Oli suddenly whispered that he felt sick. Something about a shell-food dinner the previous night. I was a tad perplexed, since this came completely out-of-the-blue.

A short two minutes later and Oli made a dramatic exit from the room, hand clapped over his mouth. The Korean sales force all clapped as well, thinking that it was all part of the act. Excellent anti-marketing, they all probably thought. Actually, I did too.

About half an hour later, a green-faced Oli re-appeared, on the arm of the president of the company, who looked similarly off-colour. He suggested that I send Oli back to the hotel immediately. So, despite Oli's protestations that he now felt a lot better, he was despatched back to the hotel, with his tail firmly between his legs.

I then tied up the meeting and left feeling that something was not quite right. The mood of the meeting had changed perceptibly after green Oli had returned.

It was only later that day when I returned to the hotel, that I was told the whole story by a sheepish Oli. Apparently, he had left the meeting room, rushed down a corridor, found the toilet room and had dived in… only to discover that all the cubicles were occupied. In desperation, he had decided that the sink would have to do. A sweaty and noisy minute later, he realised that he had 'covered' a toilet bag, toothbrush, razor and everything else within vomiting range of the sink. Not nice.

A cubicle door had then swung open slightly.

Oli spotted the movement, thought that his luck was in and had dived into the small, dark recess. He then threw up again… all over the president of the agency, who was about to leave his sanctuary. The man's suit trousers and shoes were ruined. Much confusion followed and then lots of tuts about the mess in and around the sink.

We both reckoned that this had pretty-much cooked our goose when it came to future business with this agency.

Now comes the odd bit.

In the months that followed, bookings actually increased, almost to the point where targets and sales figures went off the chart.

When I next talked to the president of the agency a year later in London, he asked very politely how Oli was, smiled and said nothing like that had ever happened in his agency before. He added that he would never forget Oli or our company.

He had even told his entire sales force the story with the result that they had instantly warmed to Oli, for some odd reason, and had started funnelling every possible booking our way.

Now, I am not saying that sales people should throw up all over company presidents to ensure being remembered, but I hope you get my point.

Steps THREE to SEVEN...

A few more practical pieces of advice to the budding, postmodernist anti-marketeer.

   3 Always allow the customer to interrupt, question and be part of the whole selling

thing. Encourage participation and criticism, especially criticism. Let the client 'breathe'. Never just drone on and on. It just wastes time, energy, breath and leaves everyone exhausted

4 **Listen carefully… and adapt**. If the client/customer/agent is not interested in something, then stop and change tack. Never push against a brick wall of disinterest. Move onto something else. Another product. Another possibility

5 If the client really does not want or need anything you have to offer, then immediately give up. **Never flog a dying horse…** you will only make yourself totally objectionable. People are never suddenly persuaded if they really do not want anything that you have in your bag of tricks. Finish your coffee and get to your feet…

6 **Be easy-going, funny and non-pushy**. Make it all very relaxed and non-threatening. Even talk about other stuff. Forget the sale for a bit, treat it as if it does not matter, because in the grand scheme of things, it really does not! Talk books, movies, sport, fashion and television. Anything that takes your fancy. Just avoid selling.

7 **Do something truly different on a personal level.** We are not quite back to red noses and vomiting. But be different in a non-dramatic way. By saying you have played tennis at

Wimbledon, had a trial for Manchester United, written a novel, appeared on television etc. But do not talk about yourself too much – try to get the customer/client to participate with a few tales of their own

So, in total, seven simple anti-pointers.

Be Plain - Remembered - Breathe - Adapt – Dying horse – Funny - Different

And now – the heavy stuff

Now we can start seriously building a rickety tower of anti-selling. What follows is a slightly flippant set of markers for the anti-sales person off to a meeting, much like the one in Korea with Oli and his toilet drama.

- **Never arrive early**

- **Try to arrive 5 minutes late**

- **Never arrive exactly on time (except in Japan)**

- **Be ultra-courteous to the receptionist and thank him or her for every small nicety**

- **Say something <u>bad</u> about the agent's office décor.**

- **NEVER talk about business at the start**

- Talk initially about sport, art, culture, books, politics etc.

- Know something about the agent's country and talk about it enthusiastically. Anything. A famous writer, politician, composer, rock star, sporting icon, statue, park, sculpture, building, bridge, the language etc.

- Find out the customer's birthday

- Find out what the customer likes to do outside work

- Recommend the competition a lot

- Say a few bad things about your own business

- Let your client see your meeting list of the day with all his or her competitors

- Ask the agent which of his or her competitors is the best to visit next

- Ask the agent for some 'petty' but useful information (i.e. where the nearest chemist is for headache tablets, or where you can buy stuff like chargers and plugs)

- Look tired and ready for a beer

- Invite the agent out for lunch / dinner / coffee and let the agent pay for you. <u>But don't forget to offer to pay.</u> Then offer to reciprocate when they are next in your country (or city)

- And never, ever talk about your product for at
  least three quarters of the first ever meeting
  with a possible client, even if he/she asks you to
  do so. That can wait. The worst possible thing
  you can do is turn to page one of your brochure

- If all of this fails to make a mark, resort to Oli
  tactics

Crucially, before attending any meetings (especially in
a foreign clime), devote at least a day to walking the
streets, seeing the sites, drinking in the local bars,
visiting museums, galleries and the big tourist
attractions. Spend your budget on learning about
how a country or city 'ticks', before venturing into
any meeting.

Sales and marketing people who indulge in these
tactics in the world of today, generally get the
business in the end and make genuine friends for life.
Honestly.

They are viewed as trustworthy people, who actually
like the countries or cities they are visiting, as
opposed to the ones who jet in, drone on endlessly
about their products, express no interest in the agent
or customers alike... and then jet out again, thinking
that they have done an excellent job.

To be remembered is crucial and the ones who make a
genuine effort to achieve this, will always reap the
benefits. Forget statistics, charts, targets and 'always-
be-closing'. Nowadays, this will hardly ever work.

In a way, we are living in an age of: 'never-be-closing'.

In this (or in any) industry the best way to succeed is to be trusted, liked and remembered.

Finally, a few more tricky problems to avoid at all costs

There are other issues to mess with the modern anti-sales person's head. When you have established a rapport with a client, then it is easy to slip into a number of nasty traps, which will lose you the day, no matter how wonderful or different you are, or how plain and 'normal' you look.

First, falling into your pet 'comfort zones'
For example, in the case of English language sales people, it is easy to wax lyrical about all your English programmes and studiously ignore the Teacher-Training and Junior courses, simply because you are not that certain about them and do not want to answer any tricky questions. Everyone likes to sell the stuff they know best – and it is a great temptation to concentrate entirely on the areas you are most at home with.

Second, rote learning
Many companies nowadays think that they can avoid all sales training, by using mechanical sales 'scripts'. Take telesales call centres and their hundreds of humanoid sales 'robots'. Much better to stutter, repeat and make mistakes. Lots of mistakes. Potential customers love to see the vulnerable, nervous side of the sales person.

Third, the 'passion trap'

Don't get me wrong, used in the right place, passion is a lovely word. Like with your wife, husband, partner, cat, dog, bunny, kids, football team, favourite food or drink etc. But not with sales and marketing! A client or agent will see through that immediately, simply because it is not true. In fact, I knew a PR manager once, who instantly rejected anyone applying for a job being recruited for, who said the word passion. Interviews and jobs have no place for being passionate!

Fourth, 'underselling' and 'overselling' – both just as lethal

The first underlines lack of product knowledge and self-confidence issues and the second makes the sales person sound like Arthur Daley on a bad day. Both can lead to the worst situation of all – the promise you cannot keep or the explanation that was wrong. To do either can cause heartache at both ends of the sales funnel… and possible lawsuits.

SECTION FOUR:

the 'P's, the Internet, statistics and numbers

10. confusion

This is all pretty scary stuff

...so, let us take a step back before we attempt to grapple with anything else. We have had a look at postmodernism and some of its aspects and then dipped our toe into the pond of practical issues when it comes to anti-selling – now it is time to take stock and a few deep breaths. Possibly a lie down, too.

Anti-marketing or postmodernist marketing tries to harness the wild, runaway horse of contradiction and illogicality, not by attempting to tame the beast, but by making sure it runs in the direction that we want it too. A somewhat tortured metaphor, but slightly appropriate.

The purpose of this 'guide' (as has already been outlined) is not to delve into the hidden, dark recesses of postmodernist and anti-marketing theories, but is meant to be an understandable and practical handbook, showing how postmodernist marketing and sales can be used in businesses today in all sorts of wonderful ways.

Wobbly Jelly

The Chartered Institute of Marketing (CIM) says that marketing is: *'The management process for identifying, anticipating and satisfying customer requirements profitably.'*

Round of applause. This is great... well, it was great in the past, when all those Ps ruled the marketing world and experts referred to the 'marketing mix' in hushed tones when stumped for any other answer. The only problem is that management processes are finding it increasingly difficult to cope, despite the most robust systems. Identifying what the customer wants can be a real pain with the tsunami of choice available online and globally. Anticipating his or her every move is also virtually impossible, despite the most sophisticated programmes and, as far as satisfying this fickle beast is concerned, this is almost as futile.

A potential customer has many more requirements than before. It is not simply price, availability and value ruling everything. For example, customer service before, during and after the sale is of vital importance.

So, what of the unbeatable Ps?

Well, traditionally, there were 4 (product, price, place and promotion) – marketing's equivalent of the four horsemen of the apocalypse. These acted as the foundation pillars of marketing and had to be addressed successfully, if your business was to succeed. Nowadays, there are a lot more Ps to think about. David Pearson ('The 20 Ps of Marketing, 2014) had a good stab at listing virtually every noun that begins with 'P' that could possibly exist in the business world. It was a comprehensive list and worth a mention here, simply because a vast proportion of the new generation of Ps, relate to postmodernist concepts. Ps like persuasion, partnership, perception, positivity and even pessimism, get air-play in his list.

The original Ps certainly still have relevance. It would be silly not to admit this. It is just that the whole P world has got a lot more confused and complicated with the Internet's arrival. Many more Ps have grown like weeds around the original 4, all seeking sunlight and prominence. This is probably the most difficult time for marketing people. The most difficult and… the most exciting. Marketing to the postmodernist customer has become far closer to magic than anything else, resting uneasily on the wobbly jelly of unpredictability and the human element.

Customers have become irrational creatures, who will walk from products at the merest hint of something they do not like. They do not resort to logic or sense anymore. Far more subjective things have increasing prominence. So, how do we pick our way through the weeds and achieve some kind of… anti-harmony?

11. the Internet has become a wrecking ball

It is also a constantly-changing and very unpredictable wrecking ball. First, it cannot be regulated, simply because it cuts across nations' boundaries and is the ultimate in free speech. And second, it deals with fragmented everything (customers, products etc.) at a quantum level. It is all-powerful – it rules every aspect of our lives and has become the ultimate modernist, traditional, postmodernist, marketing machine.

Chris Anderson *('The Long Tail',* 2006) argued that the Internet has levelled the playing field completely. Small and niche markets have become immensely powerful. Products can be offered and delivered online, without costly overheads and small operators can now do for free what large companies spent millions on.

Also, one product now certainly does not suit all. Gone are the days of Henry Ford and *'you can have any colour you like, as long as it's black'*. You now really can have any colour you desire and even a combination of bespoke, rainbow colours, to boot… and all delivered within a few hours.

And with this huge spider's web of communication and choice, there has been a massive increase in the amount of information, which is now available to the customer. He or she knows a lot more and can talk to others interested in the same products and discuss the merits or drawbacks of suppliers and products on a global scale at any time of the day and night... and get instant replies and advice.

Suddenly, the whole marketing game has changed. The power has switched from the seller to the buyer almost overnight. Stephen Brown ('*Brands and Branding*', 2016) put it rather nicely, when he said that consumers used to be: '*like fish in a barrel, but now are like cockroaches. We spray them with marketing and it works. Then they adapt.*' And it is the Internet that has allowed this adaptation on a grand scale.

But, as Richard Hall said ('*Brilliant Marketing*', 2009) – '*this new technology should be seen as a friend to marketeer and customer alike. It is not the enemy. It acknowledges that the customer has become smarter and knows a lot more. It has also created new demographic segments (or neo-tribes), such as Generations X, Y and Z, along with the teen and 'silver' markets, to name but a few.*'

And the fuel that powers the beast? The reason for its massive importance. Well, apart from porn and inane chatter. First, the insatiable thirst for knowledge and second, the desire to make money. We can talk about other factors, but these two are the main pillars holding up the Internet skyscraper.

Trust the Numbers

The BBC recently broadcasted a docudrama called: *'Brexit: The Uncivil War'*. Why this is important is that it highlighted the difference between the old and the new in the brutal hyper-reality of a semi-true documentary-drama.

The marketing old guard in the programme were shown to be techno-phobic dinosaurs, who still believed that marketing was brochures, posters, advertising, knocking on doors, spreadsheets and traditional segmentation etc.

The new guard said this was all redundant rubbish. Everything could be done at a computer console with access to the Internet, number crunching. Multiple market segmentation to the most minute degree across a whole tableau of issues. Knowledge of the electorate at a quantum level. Gold dust.

The new guard argued that there was now no need to leave the computer nerve-centre. No need to produce posters, banners, leaflets or knock on a single door. And no need to have expensive advertising campaigns. Just let the numbers do their work and reap the benefits.

It was both a bleak and an exciting vision of the future. According to the programme, people can easily be herded into making the 'right' decision. It was simply a matter of targeting everyone with the most appropriate information and leading them by the nose towards the desired vote.

The recent issues with *'Cambridge Analytica'* and the US elections are also a stark case in point. Mark Edwards (*'Herd'*, 2007) put it very succinctly. He said that we should forget individual 'choice'. People just copy or follow and that it is not individuality that people crave, but acceptance as a group. He said that we are a 'we' species suffering from the illusion of 'i' and that it is a misplaced notion of what it is to be human to say that everyone makes their own choices. Herd instinct guides us all. And the people who manipulate the Internet are the herd's sheepdogs.

However, this was the case back in 2007 when Hall wrote these words. The Internet environment has altered in recent years. Human herds are no longer large, easily-led groups, but have fragmented into smaller herds.

It could even be argued that these Internet herds have ceased to exist entirely as large herds, but are now sophisticated micro-herds. And who makes up these new herds? Well, other herd leaders who have their own micro-herd, which is made up of micro-herd leaders.

And so, we have all become herd leaders, because the Internet allows this. There are no followers anymore, just leaders leading other leaders! Multiple segmentation to the cellular level! A herd has become a lot of 'i's seeking other 'i's to form a 'we'… of sorts. We have changed from just being large, bland herds cantering wildly towards the next watering hole, which someone has chosen for us. Our herds have split and then split again, with some of us not bothering to go to the watering hole at all, while others have decided that attacking the lions is the best option. It is the age of the individual.

So, what can analysts do to analyse and segment all the constantly-changing factors which make up a postmodern herd of leaders trotting in different directions? Well, age, colour, religion, wealth and beliefs do not matter anymore. Whereas before, society was segmented along these lines, it is pointless to do so in this digital, postmodern age. In the past, these factors shaped your herd and gave experts something to hang their statistical hat on. It was an easy way of categorising the populace and then cracking the whip, accordingly. Marketing was comparatively simple back then. You could focus your campaign on your chosen demographic area and… count the money rolling into your bank account.

That does not happen now. Herds form and dissipate in completely different ways.

What matters is who you communicate with on Facebook, Instagram, LinkedIn, WhatsApp, WeChat, Messenger, Twitter, and Snapchat, what sort of YouTube or Spotify downloads you watch or listen to. It is what you buy online, where you buy it and what you browse that matters in today's world. You may join the online herd which shops at Primark, Domino's Pizza, Tesco's and Amazon, whilst being a member of a herd which visits the Tate Modern every month.

It truly is the age of the neo-tribe. These are seemingly random and disconnected groups, herds or gatherings of people of all ages, backgrounds, professions and religions, which the Internet has created on a vast scale. Inter-connected yet diverse; interlocked yet random; chaotic yet ordered. Neo-tribes exist everywhere on the Internet. We are all members of at least one, but most of us are members of many more, without even knowing it. It is fragmentation to a minuscule level and on a massive scale.

Take me, for example.

One totally unimportant, insignificant individual. I am a registered member of the Northampton Town official football club website - the unofficial one too. I am also signed up to: Seth Godin's pithy daily blog; the historian, Lucy Worsley's Twitter feed; the Discord and Reddit game sites, Songkick - for my kind of concerts; Easyjet for flights; the 'Who Wants To Be a Millionaire' and 'I'm a Celebrity... Jungle' sites; the Ancestry UK website; a few neo-progressive rock band sites and... the 'Pokémon Go' game site, of course. I also have my own company website (SuperCourses) with a small group of dedicated followers; as well as a modest 32 wonderful followers on Twitter, (a few) more on Linked In and masses on Facebook. My blogs regularly go viral, reaching three figures in only a few hours. Sigh. I would like to think I am pretty unique.

But then again, everyone is unique. That is why we are human, because we all have strange, weird and wonderful personalities and interests. The Internet, as previously argued, has made everyone their own segment, their own completely unique subset of a subset of a subset…

And even though statisticians can create the most sophisticated data analysis programmes ever, they still find it almost impossible to predict what the public, the customer or the voter will do next. We may think (as marketeers) that we can achieve some kind of maximum probability (as seen in the BBC Brexit docu-drama) if given all the right information, but it is still rough guesswork, at the end. We can analyse what people do, buy, vote etc. but can never legislate for human emotion, or whim.

Or can we? Enter Amazon

Amazon is a great example of how statistics can not only 'work' in predicting what people do - from the macro to the micro, but also in how such information is possibly the future when it comes to marketing and sales. A recent *'Panorama'* (UK current affairs programme) investigation into the power of Amazon left me believing that the George Orwell had got it just about right.

Amazon started purely as a mover of stuff from A to B. Logistics on a grand scale. They then moved onto pastures new and became the massive conglomerate that we all know and love today - with tentacles reaching into virtually every family on the planet. This is not necessarily a bad thing. Amazon has taken the practical use of new technology forward at a breathtaking pace. And the majority of people readily accept their 'innovations' into their lives and invite Amazon in quite happily. After all, speedy delivery on the day of purchase, a global marketplace and nearly every possible variation of every possible item available at the tap of a key, is something we have always dreamed of. Sacrificing a small amount of personal privacy is a very small price to pay for such a wonderful service.

Amazon have now moved to a new level and turned to statistical profiling in their attempts to 'second-guess' the customer. Every single piece of information is gathered, gleaned, itemized and filed away on every one of us. From what we buy, look at or browse on the Amazon site, to what we ask 'Alexa' about. Everything is recorded, filed away and used to build a profile.

What Amazon discovered from all this information gathering is that people really are extremely predictable (even the likes of myself). Every idle session perusing Amazon adds to our profiles, so that a steady stream of buying 'suggestions' can be then provided on our screens, all based on our browsing and purchasing history. It is Amazon showing us that it has our 'personal' tastes at heart. Itis not seen as 'influencing' decisions in any devious way, but in purely providing help and advice.

Leo Kelion (the Panorama reporter) said that Amazon is *'finding patterns in the noise of customer behaviour'* with its 'targeted recommendations' and that 'Adrian's Amazon' (my patch) is there to make my experience better, quicker, more targeted and easier.

The programme looked at how Amazon saw data and analytics as one of its main areas for expansion in the future. Not to dwell too much on this, but Amazon now has gone into business with its competition (Waterstones, M&S etc) and gleans customer data from customers of these companies. It has also moved into home security by linking ALEXA with the RING security service.

And with Amazon customers placing cameras and microphones in nearly every room in their houses, Amazon can gather a huge amount of data on nearly every aspect of our lives.

Then there is facial recognition, lip-reading and those 'wrist-watch' health bands which record and monitor heart beats and how far we have walked in a day. There is even something in development called 'speech-emotion detection'. Amazon knows (or will know) pretty-much everything about everybody very soon.

And now we reach AWS (Amazon Web Services) which provides developers with storage, tools and power for specific tasks when building new additions to sites, whether it be Apple, Netflix, Walmart, Sainsbury's, the UK's Ministry of Justice or the CIA…

Amazon says that all of this mighty power has been developed purely for the 'good' of the customer and that they never misuse data. And there is no reason to doubt this, especially since none of these activities are in any way devious or clandestine. Customers happily invite Amazon into their homes and use their services.

Furthermore, on a very personal note, it would be very ill-advised for me to criticise Amazon in any way since this is the prime outlet for this book. So, hats off to Amazon – best and quickest business on the planet!

Don't trust the numbers (massive contradiction coming up)

On the other hand, all this data collecting and number-crunching is still very hit-or-miss, despite all the most amazing ways that corporations can get into our daily lives. Statisticians can segment, analyse and try to understand customer fragmentation and our neo-tribes but, at the end of the day, Donald Trump becomes president, the UK votes to leave Europe, Jeremy Corbyn becomes leader of the UK Labour party and the Conservative Party win the 2019 general election in the UK by a landslide. The data, pollsters and statistics analysers all pointed to totally different results beforehand, because that is what the data predicted.

Amazon may disagree, but there is a valid argument that the modern consumer, voter, buyer have never been less understood - the ultimate irony, given the power of computerised analytics to the quantum level.

Why? Because, everything nowadays is unpredictable, illogical, risky and chaotic. There are no real rules, no real paths. We express our 'individuality' on the Internet in a totally random way. We join and leave neo-tribes every other minute for no particular reason. We change our minds at the drop of a hat, simply because we can. It might be because we saw something dramatic and mind-changing on the television, in the newspaper or on the Internet. Or it could be that we just woke up one morning and decided to do something different for no logical reason. What we think today can be different to what we think tomorrow and the day after.

Marketeers will claim, of course, that customers can still be steered in some way. We are back to that Brexit docu-drama again or the Amazon model where mass 'anticipation' of the voter/customer through the Internet is possible on an Orwellian scale.

The problem with this line of thinking is that it presupposes some sort of control over the digital universe, some way of pushing people towards a certain way of thinking. This might have been possible in the recent past but, as the world becomes more and more tech-literate and aware of multiple opinions, views and targeted manipulation, the less control marketeers have. The customer can see everything today – truth, half-truths, semi-lies, fibs, lies and massive whoppers, in all their glory. And can then tell their peers immediately on a global scale.

Amazon have realised this and so, quite openly, tell their customers of their intentions. If customers are suspicious or do not approve, then they have the option of walking away. Of course, most people do not – the lure of a massive choice on a global scale and instant speedy service are things that we cannot resist even if we acknowledge that privacy (to a certain degree) has been compromised (slightly).

The Brexit docu-drama highlighted the ways that clever statisticians can wield their wizardry to get the 'right' result, as in the UK Brexit referendum. However, in exposing this as the new way forward – the argument for statistics ruling everything in our lives, became its own condemnation.

It is similar to what scientists call 'The Observer Principle', where the act of watching something... changes results. And the public watched and learned. Anyone who sat through the Brexit docu-drama will never look at the side of a 'battle-bus' again and believe the strident promises written there. It will also treat targeted advertisements which appear on their Facebook pages with the contempt they deserve. An already suspicious public has now become a whole lot more suspicious. In a way, the programme managed on one level to spike its own guns, quite spectacularly, with its portrayal of statistical breakdowns and micro segmentation.

In a way, the Panorama programme on the way Amazon is moving towards becoming a 'data-gathering' company on a global scale, will make the man or woman in the street sit up and take notice like never before. Knowing that every single browse on an I-pad or comment in the 'vicinity' of ALEXA, has made us all a little warier and conscious that Amazon is 'listening' at all times. This will undoubtedly influence our behaviour.

Richard Hall (*Brilliant Marketing, 2009*) said that marketing has become more 'art' than 'science' nowadays and that marketeers should put away their calculators and rely far more on their feelings than on a total trust and belief in logic and statistics.

And the French sociologist and philosopher, Jean Baudrillard, added that we are now faced with *'more and more information and less and less* meaning.'

Relying on gut feeling can be both productive and unpredictable, but as Donald Trump proves, you can survive by being creative, subjective and emotive about controversial issues without any offering any sort of substantial proof. Facts and numbers are dry and boring in his world. Emotion rules the day simply because we are human and have short-term interests.

A final thought on this. Trump constantly challenges the data on climate change, despite overwhelming evidence showing that human beings are gradually wrecking our planet. The mass of information and reports are all in agreement that human behaviour is altering the planet's climate irrevocably. Trump just says that he does not believe this – there are no facts backing his argument up. He does not need them. He just tells the American people that he is protecting their jobs. And that is enough. Short-term interest wins based on limited evidence and people in America buy into this. Why bother about an uncertain future based on depressing tomes of statistics, when we have more important issues right now?

And most human beings, by their nature, prefer the illogical, emotive immediate argument to the hard, soul-less and doom-ridden prediction of an apocalyptic future which will occur whatever we do and when we are all dead anyway. We need food on the table now and a job to go to on Monday. The polar bear and the rainforest can wait.

And so we reach a frustrating impasse where the immovable object of Trump's subjectivity and the irresistible force of data objectivity sit looking at each other in a gridlocked stalemate.

SECTION FIVE:

The established pillars of postmodernist marketing

12. having a go at nailing custard to the wall

Experts, theorists, professors, doctors, thinkers, writers and deranged lunatics have all tried to harness the beast of postmodernist marketing and all its different meanings and interpretations, by utilising various tools from their metaphysical bag of tricks.

Professor Stephen Brown was pretty-much the first expert to have a go at corralling the beast, when he put forward three basic rules for postmodernist marketing at the end of the 90s. All three tackled the bedrock of the entity by looking at: the idea of change (concentrating on the 'new' and the 'complex'; by examining the sub-discipline of consumer research and by assessing marketing practices and their relationship with research methodologies. He also went a step further by claiming that postmodern marketing should reject attempts to impose order and working in silos. Instead, research and theory should work together with *the 'artistic' attributes of intuition, creativity, spontaneity, speculation, emotion and involvement.'*

The Holy Grail (another one), of course, is to find a plausible and believable list of pointers or markers which will explain postmodernist or anti-marketing, as slickly as possible. To find a way of categorising the whole shooting match. Which is acutely hypocritical, I know, since chaos, disorder, contradiction and confusion are, by their very nature… uncategorisable. And to breakdown postmodernism into nice little subsections, is just not what it is all about. It is the exact opposite and arguably, no longer postmodernism, but something else.

However…

Needs must where the devil rides. And anyway, it is interesting to note what experts on postmodernism perceive as the main areas - in a predominantly marketing context. And so, here is a list of everything that experts and theorists consider have an impact on marketing today in a postmodernist sort of way. Some of the explanations may be slightly bland, simplistic and generalised, but I have desperately tried not to drift into the choppy waters of meta-narratives, dialectics and the Heisenberg Principle.

Plurivalence or Pluralism
(or no rules - or something like that)

This is a good one to start with, but you need to have had several drinks to understand it. It could be argued that Plurivalence is one of the 7 Ps of anti-marketing (another set of Ps, I am afraid). The others being: paradox, prevarication, profligacy, profanity, playfulness and… phantasmagoria (yes, really). I say this with my tongue very much in my cheek. The Seven Anti-Ps of the Apocalypse. It has been argued that plurivalence is the condition where there is 'no fashion, only fashions', 'no rules, only choices', and where 'everyone can be anyone'. It is the co-existence of 'various truths' or styles which create... personal expression. It also emphasises innovation and intuition.

We are teetering on the brink here of philosophical nothingness, I know, but plurivalence should probably be viewed as a 'tolerance' of many or all styles and where marketing is pretty much open to anything.

In a very simplistic way - take the famous Guinness campaign a few years back – the one with surfers in a rough sea, loads of white horses, a nonsensical poem and a drumbeat in the background. We have art (the advertisement was shot in black and white), poetry, clever use of photography ('white horse' waves actually metamorphosing into real white horses) and that drumbeat, of course. And all absolutely nothing at all to do with the product. Or perhaps, it has everything to do with it. It is a glorious mixture of styles... and all just to sell an alcoholic drink.

Retrospection
(or using the past)

This is pretty much anything to do with the past - the retro-look, nostalgia or chronology, as it is sometimes called. Like the Mini car of the 60s being rolled out to sell 21st century clothing.   Or the Hovis ad, with a bloke in some northern town pushing a bike up a steep hill to deliver bread.   Or an Audrey Hepburn lookalike eating Galaxy milk chocolate in a vintage car somewhere near Monte Carlo.   It is the use of the past to sell the present, because there is nothing quite like the 'good old days' to stimulate a tired public into getting its wallet out.   Why it is in the field of postmodernism is a little strange - probably because it breaks down time boundaries and throws all eras and people into a confusing mix.

Self-Referentiality
(or talking about yourself)

This is an easy one.   Quite simply, it is when the marketeer takes centre stage.   Forget the customer and the product.   Just concentrate on telling the world about the marketing team and its aims and goals! Take the recent OASIS soft drinks advertising campaign.   Their campaign markets the OASIS team marketing the drink!   The billboard posters do not expound the virtues of the drink, but simply say that Joe Public should buy the product, because this will increase profits for the OASIS sales team.

Another great example is the film, 'Jurassic Park', where merchandise on the making of the film is in the souvenir shop in the film just prior to the place being flattened by a very 'real-unreal' tyrannosaurus. You do not get more self-referential than that with product placement and hyper-reality thrown in for good measure.   Thanks to Professor Stephen Brown for handing this example to me.   He describes it in his usual laid-back, laconic manner in that monumental work, '*Postmodern marketing*' (1995, p. 20):

'... *at this point in the film, the audience is viewing the film of the book of the film of the film of the book. What is more, as the book of the making of the film also refers to this scene, we are actually dealing with the book of the film of the film of the book of the film of the film of the book.*'

Then there is the old Yellow Pages television advertisement, featuring a tired, old author looking for his own creation ('Fly Fishing', by JR Hartley) in a dusty bookshop. The fictitious book is intended to show how useful the Yellow Pages is. Ironically, it actually inspired someone to go ahead and actually write a book on fly fishing by, you guessed it, a JR Hartley. Here we have self-referentiality meeting hyper-reality in a cosy mix.

Self-referentiality gets its place on a list of all things postmodern, because it messes with conformity and concentrates attention on the marketeer (or writer) and not on the customer.

Decentering

(or concentrating on peripherals, not the core product)

This is a rather nice one, since it takes a bit of lateral thinking to understand. At the core of this concept is control, dominance and uniqueness. It has been interpreted in many different ways, depending on

whether you are a philosopher, writer, marketeer or…
feminist.

Basically, if you are a modernist, then you believe
that the subject, the human being, the customer, is the
centre of attention and that everything exists to serve
his or her needs and make life better for him and her.

In postmodernism, the human being is 'decentred'
from the position of total control. It has just become
part of the 'process', where everything has similar
importance.

How on earth does this work? To answer this, I
always like to paraphrase Jean Baudrillard and his
example of the car. In postmodernism, he said that
the driver is simply a small part of the whole process.
The subject (driver) is the computer at the wheel, the
dashboard is the brain, the wheels, its way of moving
and the engine, its power source. The driver is
technically not the controlling factor, but is very much
dependent on all the other factors at play. Every part
is as important as the other parts and dependent on
them all working in harmony. So, the driver is just
part of the machine. Another cog. An important one,
but really just a machine part. The subject has become
just part of the process.

Of course, in modernism, the driver is the centre of
everything – the most important element, upon which
everything revolves.

In marketing, decentering is often interpreted like
this:

*"Decentering the subject occurs when a brand
personifies the product or service being marketed."*

A slight shift in emphasis is required here, although the general hypothesis still holds – sort of. Decentering revolves around the brand itself having more importance than the particular product or service. It is a subtle shift of emphasis. For example, we talk about 'Hoovers' instead of vacuum cleaners and 'Xeroxes' instead of copiers. These 'genericizations' occur when the product ceases to be the centre of the selling process. It is the brand which assumes prominence because of its dominance in the market place. The customer then labels all vacuum cleaners (no matter what the brand) as Hoovers and all copiers as Xeroxes. Individual products are just massed together under one convenient and well-known brand heading.

So, what does this actually mean in practical terms? Well, on a very basic level, it must be very gratifying to the Hoover company that most people in the world refer to all vacuum cleaners as Hoovers, or to the good people at Google headquarters that all searching on the Internet is referred to as 'googling'.

Of course, if you are a competitor, then it is virtually impossible to break into such a closed market and avoid your Shark or Dyson vacuum cleaner being called a Hoover. The product has effectively been 'peripheralised' or decentred by the dominant brand.

Another aspect of decentering directly involves the customer and something called 'uniqueness'. Put simply, how can a customer be unique when everyone is wearing / drinking / eating these brands. How can they all be unique? The consumer has just become part of the mass-produced process. No longer unique. No longer the centre, but marginalised with a million others. Take perfume or after-shave – television commercials mostly concentrate on selling their products to the rebellious individual. Wearing Dior, Opium, Marc Jacob and Hugo Boss (other brands are available), are supposed to give the wearer a certain kudos – a certain something, which is meant to make him or her unique and the centre of social attention. But, of course, the more popular the product, the less the uniqueness.

Of course, uniqueness can be still attained by a combination of brands, each customer adapting and accessorizing according to personal choice and whim. And here we have the customer as just a sum total of conflicting / contrasting brands. Decentred much like Baudrillard's car.

Finally, there is the decentering of the brand itself, because it is forced to change from its original 'meaning', due to cultural, moral, medical or ethical reasons. Take Marlborough, John Player or Dunhill. At the start of their lives, the three brands were associated with smoking and tobacco products.

These competing brands were sold to a smoking public on the ticket of expressing individuality and personal choice in the guise of puffing away on a cigarette. Smoking became synonymous with freedom of choice, manliness, the outdoors, cowboys and… individuality.

But then the brand evolved. Because it had to. Clearly, when doctors began talking about the serious health dangers of cigarettes, the brand had to shift its dynamic quite drastically.

So, creative marketeers reacted by slowly removing the core product from the centre, but retaining the brand dominance. The customer began to think of all wide-open spaces in America as Marlboro' country, or to associate John Player Specials with racing cars and Dunhill with tweed jackets and riding boots, but crucially, not with cigarettes.

The brand had gradually altered from tobacco products to something completely different. It had developed into a whole new range of products, which were as far from smoking as was physically possible. The core product had been decentred from the whole process.

Although the three conglomerates still produce cigarettes, they are now far more associated with a fragmented range of products, from clothing to perfume, denim jeans, accessories, bags, scarves and even jewellery.

We have reached a situation where the original product has been deliberately 'peripheralised' or decentred to the extent that many 21st century consumers do not even know that cigarettes etc. were the main products, when the companies where initially created.

Reversal

(or the customer has become part of the selling process and is not just the end bit)

This concept is of increasing importance in a world where brands mean so much. The simple premise is that the roles of the marketeer and the consumer have changed, so that it is the consumer who has assumed the role of 'brand ambassador', aligning his or her beliefs to reflect that of the brand.

Long ago, when modernism ruled the waves, and capitalism dominated thinking, it was production which was of greatest importance, because it had to be. After two world wars, the emphasis had to be on mass-production.

But, put simply, with the gradual decline of heavy industries like steel, coal, cars etc. and with the advent of shopping malls, self-service and do-it-yourself, it is consumption which has assumed pre-eminence.

We are now a consumer-led society.

Production and consumption were initially seen as direct opposites. Modernists believed that it was the products which defined human beings. Postmodernists sought to break the shackles of restraint and free human beings from being just the end-product of the process. A consumer-led society relies on the consumer dominating the production process.

A few simple examples: just walk into a KFC, IKEA, or most pizza restaurants. It is the consumer who is given the basic materials and then constructs the products to his or her pleasing. It might be a salad from the salad buffet or it might be a flat-pack wardrobe from IKEA. It is the consumer who leads the process. Society has become dominated by consumers doing the work – pumping petrol at self-service petrol stations; using the self-service tills in supermarkets; even being part of 'reality' television.

It is the consumer who now is of prime importance, not the producer.

Even the creation of such knowledge platforms as Wikipedia rely totally on the consumer to produce the finished article.

However, it was Alvin Tofler (*'The Third Wave'*), who introduced us all to something called 'prosumption', where both production and consumer jockey side-by-side in contented union.

Tofler argued that the whole process of 'activating' the consumer to becoming a vital part in the production process, has created the 'prosumer'.

After all, 'McDonald's consumers are now expected to serve as their own waiters, create their own meals and dispose of their own dirty plates at the end of the meal. All the 'producer' does is heat the desired choices up in record time and hand it over a counter to the consumer. He or she does the rest.

The Internet is dominated by the prosumer. Everything on Facebook, Snapchat, Instagram and YouTube relies almost totally on the consumer providing the input. The consumer has become the producer - the 'prosumer'.

This is comparatively new concept, which many businesses recognise, but fail to understand or utilise properly. Take the recent collapse of the travel agent, Thomas Cook. Their model was brilliant for the last half of the 20th century, when people booked in High Street travel agencies, loved the 'package' holiday and had limited or no access to the world of the Internet.

But the modern holiday-maker can now do virtually everything from his or her laptop and mobile phone at home. From booking airline tickets, reserving seats planes, to hotels and car rentals at the other end, the consumer can construct everything exactly to his or her specifications and tastes. A travel agent is no longer necessary or needed.

The problem with Thomas Cook was that even though they realised that online bookings were eating into their core business, they failed to adapt, refocus, evolve and recognise that this new type of consumer / prosumer existed. The result was empty High Street outlets, rising debts and eventually going out of business.

Then there is Coca Cola. There is always Coca Cola. They are a shining example of so many things.

Let's look at just one: Coca Cola 'Freestyle'.

This variation from the Coke stable applies to a new range of vending machines that Coca Cola has developed. These are vending machines of the future. No longer are they just devices for delivering a standard can of Coke to a thirsty customer on almost every street corner.

Coca Cola 'Freestyle' allows the prosumer to create his or her own drink exactly to his or her own specifications. If a cherry-flavoured Coke, light on carbohydrates, potassium and sugar is desired - then individualise by pressing the appropriate buttons. The machine is simply loaded up with ingredients awaiting the prosumer to mix and create!

If a standard Coke with no sugar is desired, then press again. There are literally millions of variations possible. And the vending machine will remember the particular prosumer the next time he or she visits and will offer the same drink without the button pressing. This really has become the ultimate in prosumer choice.

The customer has become the vital element in the creation of the product. Computerisation, digital memory and almost infinite choice have turned the whole process onto its head and given the consumer the ultimate power. And so, we enter the age of 'prosumption'.

Paradoxical Juxtaposition
(or mixing styles, cultures or timelines in a hotchpotch of contradictions...)

This is one of the juiciest aspects of postmodern marketing. It basically justifies marketing managers reacting impulsively, emotionally, illogically and on whim, whenever the occasion demands it. It is slotting the 'human' element into the mix when marketing 'landscapes' change suddenly – allowing marketing and sales managers to act 'in the moment'. It is the sidelining of rules and guidelines. This is as raw as it gets and has been perceived by many as the heart of the postmodernist condition.

'One of the most important characteristics of the postmodern world is the juxtapositions of

contradictory emotions, regarding ideas, senses and commitments of everyday life.' (Cova,1996).

So, this is the consumer messing with styles, cultures, genres and anything that takes his or her fancy. Art deco furniture rubs shoulders with expressionist paintings, punk haircuts, Gucci handbags and tweed jackets. It is mix-and-match on a grand scale. No rules. There are so many examples of paradoxical juxtaposition in marketing nowadays, especially posters and television commercials. From Russian abstract expressionist paintings advertising Coca Cola, to almost any Guinness advertisement.

Hyper-reality
(or dabbling in fantasy worlds)

Strangely, I feel most at home with this aspect of postmodernist marketing. Put crudely, it occurs when fantasy and 'unreality' intrude into the real world. Like Disneyworld in Florida, the city of Las Vegas or Harry Potter World. Reality takes a back seat and the customer indulges himself in his wildest dreams or nightmares. It is fantasy stuff. Unicorns, aliens, magic rings and Northampton Town winning the FA Cup in FIFA '21.

We happily enter these make-belief worlds, simply because they seem a lot nicer than the real world we are living in. Just watch the film *'Ready Player One'*, enter the online world of *'Second Life'* or play the GPS-driven, augmented-reality game, *'Pokémon Go'*.

Some have called the postmodern era, the age of the 'spectacle' where we really do not know what is real and unreal any more. Here we have multiple worlds of image and illusion, where visual stimulation is all important and where the 'truth' of reality takes a back seat. It is also the marketing person's ultimate dream and possibly, the future of it all.

So much can be done nowadays to get the potential customer's attention in a massive variety of amazing hyper-real ways. Perfume, shampoo and deodorant advertisements particularly rely on lavish hyper-real backdrops, simulations and graphics. Opium, L'Oreal, Lynx, among others, frequently dip their collective toes into an expressionist, digitally-unreal world, to startle the customer into remembering the brand. Just watch any car commercial... or even the recent AA (Automobile Association) advertisement where a 'real' car mechanic appears in the surreal, bizarre, fiction world of the TV series 'Red Dwarf', to repair the spaceship's engine on some godforsaken planet on the other side of the galaxy in a far-off future.

Fragmentation
(or the dividing and subdividing of brands)

This is the multiplying of products, brands, products etc. in an amoebic nightmare (or dream). Just more and more sub-brands breaking clear of the initial brand. For example, toothpaste. In the past, it was just a battle of brands (Sensodyne, Gibbs, Colgate etc). Then came fragmentation. Colgate, for example, now has five or six variants of its own toothpaste. There is one for whiteness, another for extra-whiteness, another for enamel-protection, another for gum kindness etc. And then there is Colgate TOTAL, which takes us full circle. All sub-brands competing against one another and yet fighting the same battle. Sensodyne, Arm and Hammer and all the other toothpaste manufacturers have followed suit, of course, which now means that we have hundreds of brands all essentially selling the same product, under a mass of different labels.

Fragmentation basically means that a single product or reality has been divided or broken up multiple times. The result is a mixed jumble of 'experiences' which face the consumer, offering a huge, confusing variety of choice.

De-Differentiation
(or messing with 'high' and 'low' culture)

In traditional marketing, 'differentiation' meant targeting specific segments of a market with specialized products... in two distinct ways. First, it was the subtle altering of a product to gain more of a mass appeal. And second, it was the deliberate creation of a product to appeal to a particular segment of the market. Both were aimed at reacting to the foibles and idiosyncrasies of a fickle marketplace, where the customer's needs and wants were king.

'De-differentiation' is slightly different. It is mostly concerned with an 'erosion' of what modernists labelled market and brand segmentation.

This 'erosion' has several different meanings. First, it is the erosion of traditional boundaries between competing businesses in order to create working partnerships and collaborations. In a crowded or diminishing marketplace, it is far more productive to work together, than against one another's interests. So, boundaries can be broken down or eroded, to create strategic alliances.

It is also erosion on a much more micro-level. The boundaries in modernist society, which defined individuals and institutions beforehand, have been eroded to such an extent that traditional market segmentation has become almost impossible. This aspect has sometimes been labelled 'mission drift', in particular when economies have changed over time to create a completely different set of segmentation 'rules'.

On a very practical level, this erosion of beliefs, cultures and traditional boundaries are commonly described as a 'blurring of high and low culture', where social and cultural genres mix to create a mish-mash of styles - where an opera singer might advertise a comparison site, or where bits from 'The Nutcracker' are used as background music to a Cadbury's fruit-and-nut chocolate bar.

It is the putting together of total opposites – high culture such as: ballet, opera, classic literature, art, Shakespeare, expensive brands etc. mixing with low and popular culture, such as: pop music, supermarket food and household products, which generally cater for the masses. In a postmodernist age, there are no boundaries anymore. It is erosion and blurring on a grand scale.

In marketing, we are faced with Ferrero Rocher chocolate pyramids at ambassador garden parties and sumptuous gold backgrounds in Dior perfume commercials, where luxury, decadence, opulence and beauty are all bundled together – a promise of the high life offered at an affordable price to the 'low life' in the street.

The postmodernist would argue that in the 21st century all traditional boundaries have now ceased to matter in any sort of practical way and that what we used to call high and low culture does not exist anymore.

Appropriation
(or playing with the brand)

Appropriation is an interesting one. It revolves around the product acquiring a certain (new) 'meaning' - after being bought by a customer, which is totally different from what the manufacturers meant for the product. Appropriation can occur when the customer gives a product a certain 'imaginary importance', making it valuable in his or her eyes. The product does not have to be unique in itself either – it can be a mass-produced item. It is, quite simply, special in some way to the individual customer, for mostly illogical, emotional and extremely human reasons.

Appropriation can be demonstrated by something called 'exchange rituals', where the product gains value merely as the result of being given or received as a gift. The product itself might not be anything special or of any intrinsic financial value, but as a gift it can be viewed as 'priceless'.

Then there the 'grooming ritual' where a product is part of a bigger process designed to make the customer feel better about him or herself. Getting ready to go out in the evening requires (for some) a lot of products and self-grooming. All these products form a vital chain in the process to making the customer feel good about him or herself. The product itself has little value, but as a link in the process it carries great importance and value.

And finally, there is the 'possession ritual' where the customer goes through his or her own very particular routine to personalise a product. For example, some customers who buy second-hand clothing will always wash the garment before wearing it, despite it being clean. It is claimed that this, in some way, 'exorcises' the spirit of the previous owner from the garment!

Another clever example concerns wine. This is how it goes – if you simply buy a bottle of red from Waitrose, which happens to be from a 'good' year, then you will probably drink it with your meal that night and not think too much about it, apart from it tasting quite nice. However, if you bought the same bottle of wine in the year it was bottled and lovingly 'laid it down' in your cellar for a few years, then it will have far greater value... in your mind. It is identical to the

Waitrose bottle in all physical ways, but completely different in metaphysical ways!

A final example could be a teddy bear. A mass produced, cheaply-made item which has absolutely no monetary value at all... and yet is priceless to a child, to the extent that losing it causes great emotional distress for days or even weeks afterwards. It is far more valuable than the identical, but unsold bear in a toy shop, because that bear has zero emotional worth. The bear only acquires worth after purchase and is then personalised with layer upon layer of illogical emotion and ... love. The bear will have more worth than the most expensive item in the house in many ways, and yet still be completely worthless financially. It has become a valuable receptor of 'memory' and a material witness to a childhood, long gone.

One other thought on appropriation. This requires us to look at production and consumption. Put very simply, most products are made by manufacturers for a purpose. To meet the need of the consumer on some scale. But, there is also the case of the product which is manufactured for a purpose, but achieves its value and status for other reasons, which are neither functional, emotional... or intended by the producer.

For example, take comics. Yes, comics. To own a particular copy or number which has never been opened and is still in its plastic wrapper-bag, or to have a wardrobe full of plastic toys (e.g. from the Star Wars and Harry Potter worlds) still in their unopened boxes, will have a much greater financial value than opened boxes, no matter how pristine the toys inside still are. These products have zero emotional or functional value, despite being created to meet the emotional and functional needs of imaginative children. They have, in a way, ceased to be toys and have become something else, which is neither functional or emotional – they have become valuable in purely financial ways. The toy inside does not matter anymore. In a way, the only thing that does matter is the state of the seal on the box! This is now the most valuable part of the product. The toy might as well just be a box containing a wad of cash, which can never be used! It has become a token of wealth and nothing else.

Sadly, this type of value can be extended to all items of 'worth'. The Dulwich Picture Gallery recently held an exhibition of Rembrandt's paintings, but because of the fear of theft, several paintings were kept in a dark, protected cellar, whilst reproductions were on display in the exhibition. We are faced with an interesting contradiction here. Should we be upset that we have paid £14 to see reproductions which are identical in all practical ways to the original? Or should we just accept this as a fact of 21st century life and move on? Most people would be appalled at not seeing the 'original' no matter how good the reproduction may be, for no logical reason except that… it is not the 'real' thing.

We have moved further down the line from handling the object carefully and not disturbing the seal. Nowadays, we cannot even see the seal – but are faced with just a copy of one!

Taking this a step further and looking at it from another angle - an original Van Gogh or a Monet is of vast financial value. That is a fact that society accepts and believes. Merely because these paintings are signed by the artist and not because they are of any artistic merit. Now I am not saying that these venerable artists did not produce good stuff – they undoubtedly did. What I am saying is that the signature has more worth than the painting.

Owning a Charles Liley (my father was an artist) will sadly not make you a millionaire overnight, more's the pity despite, in my eyes, the Charles Liley being vastly 'better' artistically and having oceans more emotional importance than any Van Gogh! Sadly, my father will never be an 'Old Master', but will simply be remembered by the world as an old schoolmaster!

So, what price value?

Picasso claimed that he settled his restaurant bills simply by scrawling his autograph on a napkin and then presenting that to the restaurateur as payment, claiming that it would have far greater financial worth than any paper money. He was not even producing a painting, but recognised that his scrawled autograph had instant monetary value. How low can you go? Art reduced to a wad of cash for well… nothing. We now seem to have reached the ideal environment for postmodernism and are stepping gingerly into Turner Prize territory! But let's leave that argument well alone, for now.

Value can also be attained in other ways. Had my father been a serial killer or won '*Who wants to be a millionaire?'*, then his paintings would assume a much higher financial value. This has, of course, nothing to do with the excellence of his paintings, but external factors have added value to his products. Owning a half-smoked cigar, reputedly puffed by Winston Churchill, will have zero practical value, but will undoubtedly have immense historical, emotional and cultural (and therefore financial) value.

Basically, being a 'celebrity' in today's world will add value to virtually anything that the celebrity does or owns.

Appropriation is something which affects our attitudes to commodities and products in ways which the manufacturer / maker / creator rarely intended and relies totally on the subjective value that society places on a product.

Pastiche
(or having a bit of fun with an 'established' or 'famous' story)

I have just read Stephen Brown's *'The Marketing Code'*. It is a wonderful pastiche of Dan Brown's *'The Da Vinci Code'*, and, as a bonus, is set in the world of postmodernist marketing.

Pastiche is the fun side of postmodernist marketing. It has also been termed the 'aesthetic manifestation' of postmodernism by experts who should have known better. It treads perilously close to the boundaries of plagiarism and copyright in that it exists as a humorous 'version' of a famous brand or 'story'. The reason why it is not plagiarism is that it openly proclaims itself as a copy of a famed original. There is no attempt at subterfuge or trickery here.

Another example is the Harvard Lampoon's *'Bored of the* Rings', which gives an alternative take on the Tolkien epic. Or (I'm blushing now) my own appalling six novels: *'The Marketeer Series'* – available at all moderate booksellers. These books switch from Le Carre and Hiassen to Pratchett and hopefully Tolkein, in a kaleidoscopic mixture of styles and genres – that is the intention, anyway.

Tom Stoppard's play, *'Rosencrantz and Guildenstern are dead'*, is a great example of pastiche, being a 'spin-off' of Shakespeare's *'Hamlet'*. You could even see Queen's *'Bohemian Rhapsody'* as a pastiche of many different genres (rock, pop, opera).

Parody
(or having a laugh, generally at your own expense)

This is linked strongly to reverse-psychology marketing. Like the Marmite campaign, where the makers of Marmite admit people hate their own product, or the Yorkie chocolate bar campaign, which triggered a landslide of complaints, because it stated that Yorkie bars were 'NOT for girls'. Parody is a great feature of postmodernist marketing, because it tries to persuade the public NOT to like or buy a product and to go elsewhere. It is having a bit of fun and poking its tongue out at itself.

I recently saw a poster for *'The Play that Goes Wrong'* in central London. The strapline was: *'All New Cast – and Even Worse!'* Not only do we have a play which anti-sells itself brilliantly, but just to add the cherry to the cake, we have a strapline which underlines how bad it is. It is using parody in its most brutal form. And the play sells out every night, of course.

Anti-Foundationalism
(or attacking the very foundations of it all)

Put simply, anti-foundationalists do not believe that there is any one belief as the 'foundation of knowledge' and that there are no universal rules or absolute truths. Anti-foundationalism has been described as both liberating and suspect at the same time in that it sidesteps authority, yet does not offer any solutions. In this way, it is not a very good argument for change... especially when it highlights contradiction and self-deprecation as a virtue.

If we look at this in a marketing context, then globalisation, the Internet and the many new worlds which are now open to marketeers, have created a market place where it is impossible to enforce a set of generalised rules. Whereas before, marketeers relied on objective knowledge, the emphasis today is far more on the subjective and uncontrollable. This has been interpreted as advocating instability and chaos on a grand scale. And certainly, some anti-foundationalists would agree that anarchy is the way forward! In practical marketing terms, anti-foundationalism has been used to label campaigns which directly attack themselves in order to make an impression on the customer. Think Marmite with its love/hate campaign and overt acknowledgement that a huge proportion of the public really despise their product.

SECTION SIX:

pet hates and Jo Public

13. the dragons' den

But old habits die hard...

It has been said many times previously in this
handbook that postmodernist marketing is fresh,
different and risky, whereas traditional marketing is,
by its very nature, rational, logical, conservative and
built along carefully-constructed guidelines.

However, it is all very well to advocate doing the
dangerous, exciting, adventurous and liberating
thing, but the reality today is that hedge-funds,
entrepreneurs and people with money to invest,
generally still only go for ventures which are tried-
and-tested, solid, logical and with carefully-plotted
financial plans.

We live in an age where most people would dearly
like to indulge in the dangerous gamble but, when
push comes to shove, the carefully-considered option
usually wins out. The old adage that you have to
speculate to accumulate sounds great, but rarely do
financiers do this, unless they have a lot of money to
fall back on, have done all their homework, or can
afford the danger of a 'gamble'.

You just have to watch an episode of 'Dragon's Den' to see this at work. The Dragons are all hard-bitten business people of the old school, who have made their stack. They can afford to sit pretty with a large pile of notes on a side table, waiting for something investable to come along. They rarely take a real risk. OK, they would quickly argue that this is not the case and could cite a few examples when a genuine risk had been taken on a great idea. But generally, they still put their faith in the traditional 4 Ps and make all decisions based on the marketing mix and established marketing criteria.

And there is absolutely nothing wrong in this. If I had a pile of money I too would cherry-pick carefully and enjoy that smug feeling of superiority as I surveyed the people begging before me.

Of course, this all leads to investment in stuff that has already proved itself in the market place, has a line of orders in the pipeline and a carefully-calculated financial plan. The hard work has generally already been done.

The Dragons come on board mostly to expand the brand merely by pumping in a little more money and by attaching their 'name' to the next campaign. They are needed, but really only as the final stepping-stone to the big bucks. Small-time entrepreneurs, who are not accountants or good with numbers, are generally dismissed without a second thought. It is no use having the possibility of a fantastic product with the Dragons - you have to have a solid marketing plan, financial stability and a draw full of future orders.

There is not much room in the Den for creativity, individualism and cleverness without the four Ps being firmly hammered into place, beforehand.

I know I am being a little harsh here and for that I apologise. However, it would be refreshing to have a little more risk and danger in the Den, with the Dragons putting their money behind an idea which had not yet proved itself in the marketplace. Real entrepreneurship. It would also be nice to have a Dragon in there who was relatively young and who had made his or her fortune in the digital market-place and knew how things ticked online.

The Dragons are great examples of traditional modernist marketeers

'Trunki' suitcases for children was turned down by all the Dragons despite it being a great idea and not much else. The financial plan was riddled with anomalies when presented to the Dragons, who refused to take that step into a postmodernist scenario, where gut instinct and a calculated risk were required. It was too much of an untried gamble and so the Dragons all walked away. Had the Trunki people returned to the Den a year later, the Dragons would have been queueing up to invest.

Conservatism is the easy route to follow. It was the marketing policy for such giants as Marks and Spencer's, Next, British Home Stores and even Woolworths. The people that ran these big corporations tended to rely on tried-and-tested marketing methods, especially in bad times. They drew in their wings, battened down the hatches and hoped to ride out the storm by concentrating on established core markets and by shedding the risky products. The Ps were rigidly adhered to. The marketing mix was the Bible and a variety of ancient matrices were sacrosanct. Time stood still when it came to developing new products and exploring innovative marketing. And the result – stagnation, decline and eventual closure. That policy might have worked in the past, but certainly not in the digital, postmodern marketing market-place.

The whole point of postmodernist marketing is to do something different or remarkable and to look at the world from another angle, especially when things are not going well.

Niantic opened the door to something completely new in the gaming industry. It offered the public something that they would never have dreamed of in a month of Sundays with the augmented reality game, Pokemon Go. Primark would have seemed a suicidal venture 20 years ago with a clothing market already creaking at the seams and High Street stores going bankrupt almost every week. People said the computer would never catch on and that Facebook was a daft idea. Mobile phones that did 'everything' were laughed at and the concept of Amazon, with its amazingly quick delivery service, was considered unworkable. All were initially met a wave of scepticism and doubt.

Large businesses like French Connection, Lego and ironically, Marks and Spencer's very recently, have embraced change. Real change. Dangerously risky change.

M&S announced that they would concentrate more on food in their stores – a dramatic change from the traditional image of it being a practical, middle-of-the-road store, where middle-aged people bought socks, underpants and jumpers. They then had the innovative idea of amalgamating their 'gourmet' food with a delivery company.

Lego faced 'the end' a few years ago... and then a forward-thinking director introduced pre-packaged building sets, super-hero expansions.... and crucially, the Lego 'person'. It is now claimed that there are more Lego people in the world than there are actual people. This was seen as a somewhat desperate move when it came out, since the core product of Lego was the small plastic brick, not the little person with the removable head. It was a massive risk – but it paid off, because people had faith in the man with the risky idea.

And ignore the public too

Why? Because people can only comment on what they know, not what they don't, so they will naturally only vote for the current stuff on the shelves which they know and like. Change is a dangerous word to the customer. It is generally frowned upon. Changes in store layout, product-lines, upgrades and even packaging are always disliked by suspicious customers, who are unsettled by what they do not know. Consumers are a conservative bunch, who generally only buy what they understand and trust.

There are many examples. Lovers of Microsoft XP hated VISTA, because it was different. Apple have always had problems selling their new concepts (e.g. the removal of the button at the base of their mobile...as well as the headphone socket). People generally hate the new or different, because it is the shock of the unknown. They like tried-and-tested paths which they have got used to.

A great current example is 'self-driving' cars. The technology is sound, but the person-in-the-street still hates the thought of putting his or her life into the hands of a computer. It seems dangerous and wrong on a massive scale, despite the fact that most aircraft take off and land nowadays almost totally by computer with minimal human 'help'.

It takes time to change people's minds and make the dangerous and bizarre, the norm. Businesses have to push against the grain and a possible initial decrease in sales to take the next step in technology. It is risky, but to do nothing is even riskier.

Of course, taking the risk and being dangerous does not come without its pitfalls. The most devastating example of this was the Boeing 737 Max. Experts heralded these planes as the next step in aviation – but unfortunately, its computer system failed catastrophically twice in the first year with appalling results and many deaths. Pushing the boundaries does not come without danger and possible failure, especially in areas where computers really do have the power of life and death.

The magic combination, of course, is to have a great new product which has no teething problems, an enthusiastic and innovative marketing team, a wonderful marketing and financial plan and a massive sack of money behind the whole thing. That rarely happens, of course. Usually, you have one or two of these ingredients and then have to 'fly by the seat of your pants' for the first few years.

What is needed is perpetual resilience, belief, patience, trust, a steady hand at the controls, never listening to the customer (or the Dragons) and boasting wildly how well it is all going, whenever asked.

Above all, you need perseverance and total belief in the idea, no matter what the statistics say. Of course, it can all still come tumbling down – that is the delicious unpredictability of postmodernist marketing.

14. swatting SWOT

(a minor digression on a very personal pet hate)

And never use SWOT diagrams either.

Another hate to the growing list. Why? Because SWOT is a poor attempt to objectivize and analyse a very subjective set of parameters. It could be argued that it is a relic of a traditional marketing past long gone and that it has become a sort of comfort pillow that companies bring into play when there is a free afternoon, not much to do and a big empty room.

In theory, it is a really good way of getting down all the good and bad points of a business onto a flipchart. It is a great starting point. Four nice boxes gauging the current 'mood' of the company. And, if you are feeling particularly adventurous, these sections can be subdivided into internal and external factors, so that 4 becomes 8 and a slightly more rounded analysis of what is going wrong within and without the business.

Staff generally laugh at this point.

Why? There are several schools of thought on this.

You could go down the road that Erhard Valentin did, back in 2005. Basically, Valentin argued that SWOT has 'shallow theoretical roots' leading to 'banal or misleading results'. He further claimed that not everything in a business can be categorised into straight-forward, black and white, favourable or unfavourable, bullet-pointed lists.

Valentin also made the very valid point that most elements of a business are neither good or bad. They should be seen as probably both and neither, at the same time. He saw SWOT as essentially a jumble of ideas and thoughts which lacked any criteria or prioritization.

His alternative, DOE (Defensive/Offensive Evaluation strategy) relied far more heavily on a structured theory which examined the 'internal and 'external contexts' of a business. So, what does this mean? Well, Valentin started by looking at something called 'vulnerability probing' as part of his 'defensive evaluation'. This involved assessing the business's 'resource deployment' and effectiveness. This was set against factors which affected revenue and costs as well as reporting on the business's competitors' in the market-place. Meanwhile, 'offensive evaluation' concentrated on something called 'pioneering', which looked at ways of taking a larger slice of the pie from these competitors.

And where does all this lead? To 'customer value creation', Valentin argued.

This state of nirvana can be reached when all areas of the business have been subjected to a rigorous DOE analysis, which involves not only the very measurable contexts (prices, cost, financing, logistics, advertising etc.), but also the more postmodern areas, such as loyalty, after-sales service, trust, convenience etc.

Interestingly, Valentin shunned the temptation to create his own diagram or table. Instead he produced something called a 'benefits profile', which summarised non-competitive threats hand-in-hand with a resources and capabilities profile. This crucially not only built a solid, factual picture of the business (financial, physical, legal, 'informational' etc.), but also included subjective aspects such as relational, reputational, as well as human needs and wants (i.e. the staff and customers). And that was DOE – an interesting and enlightening alternative to SWOT.

LaMarco and Seidel (2019) saw SWOT as being 'limited in scope' in that it does not encourage deeper analysis. They also highlighted the problem with staff who might have different views on what Opportunities, Threats, Strengths or Weaknesses are. Or, worse still, staff who may view something as a Strength or an Opportunity, whilst others see the same thing as a Threat or a Weakness.

And that, in a nutshell, is the SWOT diagram. Harsh appraisal, I know, but practically, SWOT does not really cut the mustard, nowadays. So, let us bin SWOT – a tired anachronism of a previous age.

Are there any alternatives, apart from DOE?

Enter SOAR.

It has been argued that SOAR (Strengths, Opportunities, Aspirations and Results) is a much better way of looking at a business or project, top-down. Critics might say that we are now drifting somewhat aimlessly into the waters of total subjectivity and that anyone indulging in a SOAR chart will end up with a similar list of banal ideas which are almost impossible to analyse and use in any constructive way. In other words, just another SWOT, but labelled differently.

However, it could also be argued that SOAR is a subtle modification to SWOT, because it focuses positively on 'going forward' and does not spend time on the negative areas. Gone are the Threats and Weaknesses boxes, making SOAR arguably more 'action-orientated' than SWOT. In this way, SOAR could be viewed as being more instantly-applicable to future problem-solving.

LaMarco and Seidel viewed SOAR as a vehicle for 'collaboration', introducing the very postmodern 6 'I's into the argument (initiate, inquire, innovate, inspire, imagine and implement), and encouraging staff to dream a little… which is never a bad thing.

SOAR is a modification of the SNOT diagram (very postmodern labelling here), which positioned Strengths, Needs, Opportunities and Threats, as an unlikely and somewhat tongue-in-cheek foursome. The Threats are still lurking in there, but Opportunities have changed into Needs. Not sure I want to dwell too long on SNOT, except to say that it probably should be placed under SWOT's wing, since it still concentrates mostly on the 'good' and the bad' sides of a business.

The SCORE analysis (Strengths, Challenges, Options, Responses and Effectiveness) took up the baton of positivity with the only one section vaguely hinting at negativity - the Challenges slot. But, it could be argued that SCORE is not backward-looking and also manages to cover most issues handled by SWOT. LaMarco and Seidel saw SCORE as far 'more proactive than SWOT', encouraging businesses yet again to look at the future, instead of dwelling on all those Weaknesses and Threats.

Then there is something called NOISE (Needs, Opportunities, Improvements, Strengths and Exceptions), where the needs of the staff or project are placed at the centre. NOISE is a refinement of SOAR and SNOT in that the forward-looking segments of Needs, Opportunities and Improvements are still allowed in the mix, with the acceptance that Strengths and Exceptions have roles to play as well. Again, there is no room for negativity in NOISE, except perhaps in the Needs section.

The only slightly tricky section is Exceptions, because no one instantly understands it. LaMarco and Seidel have an interesting take on this. They argue that this section 'encourages collaboration between members of the team' constructing the chart. It is there to act as a comfort pillow to lean back on when things look controversial and divisive - and should be viewed as the section for 'back-patting'. They see it as the area which shows how well everyone has worked together in the past and how this positive camaraderie can help build a new future. It should probably be labelled the 'Time-Out' section, but that would ruin the acronym completely.

What about SOPA (Strengths, Opportunities and Positive Action)? This is possibly the next rung on the ladder just above SOAR, although critics have said that 'positive action' is a somewhat woolly label, meaning very little. Enough of that.

And now we move into the truly postmodern with something called STEEPLE. Here we have other factors poking their noses into a diagrammatic breakdown. It is the natural successor to PESTLE (Political, Economic, Social, Technological, Legal and Environmental), and puts Social, Technological, Environmental, Economic, Political, Legal and Ethical matters together with equal importance. PESTLE has been expanded to include 'green' concerns, hence the additional 'E'– Ethics.

This is possibly the most popular 'concern' of the 21st century. Not just treating your customers and staff far better, but also making sure that your activities do not have an adverse effect on the planet. Most large companies are now advertising loudly how ethical they have become, even McDonalds, Starbucks and the major oil companies. All realise that helping the planet is not just good for future generations, but is also good business, since it is the younger generation (of course) which have these concerns closest to their hearts – and these are their principal markets.

The UK bakery company, Greggs, recently brought out its vegan sausage roll to highlight its ethical side. Normally, this would be a token gesture to a minor element of their target market, but with the massive increase in vegetarianism and veganism, the vegan sausage roll has become one of its best-sellers. This would have been unthinkable a few years ago.

Companies are looking far more seriously at their STEEPLE charts, probably with the Ethics slot as the major area of concern in board and staff meetings in years to come.

And, no doubt, there will be more interesting acronyms floating across the business landscape as we reach the 'roaring twenties'. There are now a whole new range of issues are jockeying for position, centre-stage… issues that had no real relevance just 20 years ago when SWOT was the way forward and businesses could play with their strengths and threats on quiet, dull Friday afternoons.

These new issues involve conservation and recycling, pollution, employee happiness, rights for employees, racial equality, website security, protection of customers' rights and personal information and saving the planet, to name but a few. Any business plan or diagram today has to have a large section which tackles some, if not all, of these issues.

15. dumbing it down to the lowest common denominator

Getting Noticed

So, what can a marketing and sales person do to tip the balance in his or her own favour, if he/she has a reasonable product, total belief, a 21st century attitude to global issues and staff and customer rights… BUT crucially not that much money to play with.

Ditch those Ps

A few rather obvious pointers for the uninitiated: first, when you have got a website up and running, you then have the prospect of millions looking at it every second. And if you have great products, which are pretty unique and ground-breaking, then surely there is a Ferrari waiting for you just around the corner?

Not so. Why? Simply, because everyone is doing the same. From big businesses to the guy in his or her back bedroom. We have all become sellers and think we have got unique stuff at great prices, which everyone will instantly be queueing up for.

It is at this point that normal marketing rules tend to break down. Product, place, position and price and sundry other Ps suddenly have little or limited meaning in this new, congested global market place. As Stephen Brown put it (*'Free Gift Inside'*, 2003): *'How do you attract customers when all the Ps in the world don't add up to a hill of beans?'*

And where do you go when everyone claims to be consumer-led and where rarity truly is rare. Grant LeBoeuf (*'Stickier Marketing'*, 2014) claimed that the real battle in the market place is for attention and that customers are less concerned with quality and the features of a product, because everything is becoming increasingly similar. Leboeuf also says that the scarcest resource in the marketplace is 'customer attention'.

Getting 'noticed' is 99% of the battle today. Ironically, getting your message out to the billions of people just a couple of taps away from your site, is an almost impossible task. Leboeuf adds that there has been such a distinct shift in the market place from scarcity to abundance that companies are having to shout much louder at potential customers just to get noticed. Most days, we are faced with a 'white noise' of information coming at us from all directions.

Your message has to be simple to be effective.

So, messages on the internet have to be sharp, clear, short, creative and simple. They also have to be different from everyone else. Nik Mahon (*'Ideation'*, 2011) said that companies now have to delve a lot deeper into their creative and 'wild' side and there is an increasing need for provocative ideas, so that customers are 'stopped dead in their tracks'. Long, logical arguments are a thing of the past. We want something that will smack us hard between the eyes.

So, what can we do? Well, marketing people would do well to keep the following at the front of their corporate minds.

Fundamentally, the public is an impatient and suspicious lot, who prefer to eat food out of buckets on the street and are usually far too busy to stop and think. They are addicted to reality television, game shows and soaps... and see football, dance and cookery shows as their only pastimes at the weekend. They rarely believe anyone and take a lot of convincing before reaching for their wallets or purses.

Harsh, but true. The public also has the patience of a three-year-old and wants everything extra-fast, or will walk.

Any messages approaching their collective brains have to be quick, punchy, easy-to-understand, rememberable and... remarkably simple. Simplicity rules the day. Being complicated, intelligent and logical mean very little to the 21st century person. We are living in an age where speaking plainly and in four-word sentences trumps almost everything.

The public fears the new

Add to the mix that the public is a conservative bunch that dislikes any sort of change and you begin to realise that the marketeer has an increasingly steep hill to climb. What the person in the street really wants is something familiar that he or she can instantly trust. Something tried-and-tested. The shock of the new is a worrying concept for the man or woman in the street. Anything 'new' and unfamiliar will be looked at with great suspicion and scepticism.

One nice example is something called the 'California Roll'. This was an attempt to bridge the gap between cultures, namely to make Americans eat more Japanese food (i.e. raw fish), which was previously considered shocking by most of the nation. Rather than try to bulldoze the health benefits of this new type of food onto a sceptical public, the marketing people thought very laterally. And so, something called the California Roll was born – something that had all the ingredients of Japanese food, but with an acceptably American ring to it… and covered in mayonnaise, of course. The US public was introduced to a new food culture - a glorious amalgam of Japanese raw fish products packaged in a way that Americans would know, understand and trust (i.e. smothered in mayonnaise). Some might argue that this is simple marketing trickery. Others would say that all marketing is trickery!

The public also has the memory-span of a goldfish.

Think Donald Trump. The man is a genius. Yes, I mean that - a modern-day, postmodernist genius, as has already been said. We may find his methods somewhat provocative, but it undoubtedly works for him.

His usage of the new media is a master-class, which all marketeers and sales people would do well to learn from. Logic, rules, careful argument and the truth have little meaning in his brave new world. What matters is the short, tough, sound-bite, which everybody can understand – even a three-year-old. Emotion, passion, contradiction and being human with all its frailties, are what matter most - Build the Wall / Lock Her Up / Make America Great.

It is not just the Donald. Think Brexit. And the simple message: 'Take Back Control'. Or the '£350 million for the NHS' on the side of that infamous bus. Does the truth matter? Not really. It has become a confusingly, subjective commodity. What matters most is to get your message out in simple English and with a powerful and rememberable punch. Shout out anything you like and to hell with the repercussions!

A minor digression on the nature of truth

Truth may be a grey area, but perception of truth does matter. This is where the real power lies. It is to be able to talk convincingly about something in a way that the masses instantly understand and crucially believe at a particular moment. Appealing to raw emotions, letting nature take its course and winning the 'moment' is where success lies. Whether it is in politics or marketing, the same is true. You tell the truth as you see it at that moment in time. Never mind what happens after that.

Politicians do this all the time, dismissing any previous adverse comments or criticisms as distortions of the real truth or just 'fake news'. The truth is what you tell now. What you spin at that moment. It is as simple as that.

That £350m message on the bus was true-ish when the Brexit campaigners initially unveiled it. It was not a completely true picture, of course, but no one really wanted to look at the big, true picture then. The public just wanted to grasp a simple concept, wave the flag a bit and shout about 'taking our country back'. Truth snippets. Simple messages.

That was why Donald Trump, Nigel Farage and Boris Johnson won their respective campaigns. They spoke a simple language that the person in the street understood. It is not meandering 'political-speak', which never directly answers any questions and confuses and bores the man or woman in the street.

Marketing and sales are the same today. Gone are long-winded explanations as to why the product is great and beats the competition hands-down, to be replaced with short, pithy soundbites - Adidas and: 'Impossible is Nothing'; McDonald's and: 'I'm Lovin' It'; Nike and 'Just Do It'. No long-winded promises or claims – just nice, snappy phrases. Truth of a sort, because they mean nothing.

Simplicity of message and language are fundamental to a 'truthful' political or sales campaign. We live in an age where brevity is everything and where boredom, incomprehension and suspicion are the biggest enemies. Make it short and simple has never been more appropriate.

And sometimes your version of the truth does not even require words, which is brilliant if you have a global audience speaking a mass of different languages. Pictures increasingly suffice in the market place of today. The Internet's prime marketing weapons are increasingly becoming smiley emoticons, cartoon cats and dogs, and throwaway memes. Instagram rules the day! Anything to dumb it all down to the lowest common denominator.

SECTION SEVEN:

a vision of an anti-marketing future

16. chasing dittos

Back to that Ditto hunt at the very beginning of this handbook, because Pokémon Go is a brilliant example of marketing possibilities in this new digital age

Yes, it is more on *'Pokémon Go'* now and its relevance to the grand scheme of things. But, before you flick straight to the end of this section, have a think about the excitement of catching a Jigglypuff outside your local pub and the reasons why grown adults would run around town indulging themselves in this pursuit. Have a think about the incredible technical advances that have made this game possible and... have a think about the marketing possibilities. Now continue reading, or go to the next section a lesser person!

'Pokémon Go' is an online game – in fact, it has been claimed that it is the biggest interactive, real-time, augmented or mixed reality, 'mobile' game in living history. The beauty of it is that it uses existing smartphone platforms to drop the Pokémon universe into our lives. It is not quite virtual reality, because you cannot interact with the beasties crawling around your screen, but it is pretty close to it.

So, you can see these 'monsters' on the camera function of your phones as they prowl supermarket aisles, station platforms and in your bedrooms. They are, quite literally, everywhere in the real world - at least, everywhere where there is a GPS location. In mountains, jungles, deserts, remote islands, on planes and even on ships miles from land. Everywhere.

Why is all this remotely important?
Simply because it is pure anti-marketing gold. A way of making more money than you could ever hope to dream of. It is hyper-reality, neo tribes, juxtaposition, de-differentiation, retrospection, parody, 'self-referentiality', fragmentation and even anti-foundationalism, all rolled into one absorbing and addictive game. It is the epitome of postmodernism. Even Donald Trump has been seen playing the game! And you don't get more postmodernist than the Donald trying to trap a 'Lickitung' in The White House gardens.

Plus… it is claimed that it also has health benefits (being a great way to burn calories off by walking in circles all day and night) and is known to have aided people with psychological and social problems. So, the ethical crowd are happy with the game as well – an added bonus.

It currently makes about 1.6 million dollars a day through direct revenue from its 26 million players worldwide, who buy treasure chests of gold coins through in-game purchases. And it has already surpassed all other popular mobile games as a money-spinner. Apple and Samsung have seen purchases of their mobile devices leap as a direct result of the game. Shops, cafes, restaurants, hotels, pubs and even churches have advertised themselves as 'Pokestops', where players can stock up on AR resources, while enjoying more tangible wares of the 'real' world. Even the tourist authority - '*Go London*' has sponsored 'Pokestops' for a limited time in central London. Some entrepreneurial pubs and cafes have offered discounts if players can prove they are at a certain level in the game. And restaurants and cafes with 'slow footfall' have 'lured up' 'Pokestops' near their restaurants to encourage players to eat while they play.

There is even a helicopter company in the USA, which specializes in '*Pokémon Go*' tours, where players zoom from one location to another to catch rare beasts, or take part in organized raids without being constantly stuck in traffic.

And then there are the usual spin-offs. The merchandise - from t-shirts and badges to books and fluffy toys. And we should not forget other Pokémon games on different platforms which encourage 'Go' players to invest in such additional devices as the 'Nintendo Switch' console, for example.

There is a Pokémon movie out, as well, ('*Detective Pikachu*'), which is doing for Pokémon what the *Lego Movie* did for the sale of small, plastic bricks.

There are 'Facebook', 'WhatsApp', 'Discord', 'Silph Road' and 'Reddit' fan groups, where information and general banter is exchanged online and where competitions, 'raid-trains', walking routes and pub nights are planned. There is even romance (both in the real and unreal world!).

And players are from all walks of life, genders, ages, backgrounds and beliefs - not just nerdy kids. Ironically, most players are adults, simply because the statistical side is too much for the average kid, who just wants to battle things. Your closest allies might be (real world) accountants, mountaineers, lawyers, salesmen, doctors, bus drivers and even TV celebrities.

Niantic (the company that owns the game rights) has created a massive online community of willing, enthusiastic and dedicated 'addicts', on a global scale. It knows its rough age demographic too – since the original form of the game became famous in the late 80s /early 90s. So, Niantic anticipated a huge number of potential players being in the 25-40 year old category – players with access to bank accounts and credit cards.

Niantic is also master of the 'leak'. This happens when there is an update in the offing, with new monsters being unveiled, or a new 'generation of monsters' being announced. It 'accidentally' lets slip 'hidden' data on 'updates' and releases, which are discovered very quickly by 'data-miners' of the game. This always causes a frenzy of excitement and anticipation in chat groups. It is somewhat similar to a release of a blockbuster like a 'Harry Potter' or 'Star Wars' movie. Lots of jaw-dropping trailers and then a midnight release. It all builds the excitement and increases the buzz.

Players can also 'talk' directly to the game developers via the game. If you have an idea on how to improve the game (or a criticism) you can talk to a 'real' person and get an answer. Niantic also (reputedly) listens to their players' ideas and have acted on good recommendations to improve the game making players feel as though they really are part of the game development process and not just the end product.

As for the monsters in the game, they are mish-mash of languages, parody and humour. It is a glorious melange. For example, there is a thing called 'Kabuto', which is a crab-like creature in the game ('kabuto' actually means Samurai helmet in Japanese); a 'Gardevoir' (clearly French influence here). There are anagram jumbles like 'Ekans' and 'Arbok' (I'll leave you can work these out); there are 'Luvdiscs', 'Jigglypuffs' and 'Blisseys' – all humorous parodies of what a fearsome monster should look like.

There is even something which Niantic has named a 'Lickitung', which gets its fame from being a 'banned' word in the game, because it sounds lewd and naughty. But it still exists, poking its tongue out at not just the players, but at its creator, Niantic, as well.

And finally, there are what Niantic call, the 'Alohan' variant of monsters in the game - which again is Niantic having a joke at the expense of its own creations, giving beasts silly wigs or elongating monsters to daft proportions. A lovely tongue-in-cheek pastiche of the original Pokémon monsters.

As for the marketing - there are numerous 'special events' to keep the wheels of income turning over. These generally take the form of three-hour, monthly 'community days', when a particular beast has centre-stage. Millions of Pokémon players hit the streets enmasse to bag critters and hopefully get the 'shiny' version. There are also ticketed festivals held in specific locations (e.g. Chicago, Dortmund, Tokyo) over a period of 4 days or so and where upwards of 100,000 players can jet in and take part. At 25 euros a ticket, this is another source of instant revenue.

There is also a lot of walking, because beasts are all over the place and are constantly spawning and despawning, so you can quite literally walk in slow circles around a town or park and meet up with different creatures all the time.

Of course, players need all sorts of stuff in their armoury to get as many monsters as they can. Extra Pokeballs, incubators for eggs etc. And this is where Niantic has the genius touch. To get adequate numbers of these items, you need gold coins. And to get these… get your credit card out.

Strangely, there is no direct advertising allowed within the game itself. None whatsoever, despite a conservative estimate of a possible 6 billion views, should Niantic decide to go down this lucrative route. The potential earnings from this source would be similar to revenue earned during 'hotspot' times on popular television channels.

And when TV shows like 'The Big Bang Theory', 'The Simpsons' and even computer games like 'Minecraft', 'Civilisation' and 'Grand Theft Auto' mention Pokémon, we have genuine hyper-real 'crossover'.

And that is *Pokémon Go* – a game which encompasses everything that the digital, unreal, hyper-real world can offer marketing, with health and social benefits thrown in, as well.

It has been copied, of course, (there is already a Jurassic Park variant out there as well as a Harry Potter game) as this market fragments into multiple spin-offs, using the same, but enhanced, AR technology.

And to top it all, there are now (naturally) Pokémon theme parks, along the same lines as Disney, Harry Potter or Lego, where fans can meet up and enjoy a day of Pokémon-inspired rides and dance with underpaid students dressed up as Pikachus.

We can all live the unreal Pokémon dream.

Of course, this is just one example from the rich tapestry of augmented reality possibilities available now.

A brave new world

The developers of 'Pokémon Go' freely admit that the game dynamic is just the first stepping-stone to an amazing future. Current AR technology has been described by Niantic as a 'crude parlour game', since (for example) the hyper-real monsters in 'Pokémon Go' are merely 'laid' onto the real world, via our mobile phones. The next step will be making these 'cartoon' beasts interact 'properly' with the real world - like jumping fences, disappearing round corners or hiding behind cars. Mobile phones will also cease to be the medium, it is thought, to be replaced by high-tech,

AR-receptive glasses so that players really can submerge themselves into the hyper-real world.

It will not just be for playing games either. You will be able to buy train/theatre/plane tickets through these glasses, get historic data of the area you are travelling through, receive information on shops you happen to be passing and be able to buy stuff online from real stores around you.

You will be able to wander the streets of cities on the other side of the world, while walking around your back garden at home. You will be able to explore other planets and even swim in the deepest oceans, while buying a pack of Weetabix or a bunch of bananas in a supermarket. You will be able to sit in a hyper-real seat at the Cup Final or be with the first astronauts as they step onto the surface of Mars. All through a pair of glasses. Everything will be designed to create the complete, immersive experience.

And advertisers will be everywhere as well.

It is said that every spare 'patch' of untouched digital ground (or air) will be up for grabs. So, the sides of buildings, monuments, bridges, churches, trees, roads, mountains and even clouds in the sky, will all be sponsored by Coca Cola, Kit Kat, Nike, Sony, Samsung...

Logos, straplines, photos of products will be, quite literally, everywhere. We will be walking in a world where nowhere is safe from the marketeer! Just have another look at the movie, 'Blade Runner', and you will get an idea of how our hyper-real future could be.

This is obviously both good… and bad.

There are many counter-arguments about living in a world like this but if, as a result of digital advertising, all 'physical' advertising is removed completely, because it would be redundant in this new age, then we would truly have the choice of just switching our 'receptors' off (or restricting the information), so we could enjoy a 'clean' physical environment again, free of all physical advertising like billboards, posters etc.

It is thought that when 5G and then 10G and 100G are developed, this kind of technology will make such dreams (nightmares) a real possibility. There are already projects underway, which are exploring these new boundaries (e.g. *'Codename: Neon'* and *'Tonehenge'*).

SECTION EIGHT:

Anti-marketing in the workplace

17. so, where does all this fit into postmodernist marketing and sales today?

An age of shifting sands

Well, first, there are no governing rules for all the technological advances we are experiencing, as yet. It really is an age of shifting sands, where new ways of expressing yourself digitally, occur on a daily basis. You can say almost anything. Be anything. You can create your own truth and get it out to millions within seconds. You can be a professional with millions of dollars and countless followers behind you, or you can be an amateur with no budget at all, a handful of followers and with just a few things to sell on e-bay.

So, there it is. The world of digital internet marketing in a nut-shell, with everything resting a little uneasily, on five cyber conditions:

Brevity
Simplicity
Getting noticed and remembered
Realising that your truth is the only truth

Acknowledging that reality is rather subjective

But, as I keep saying, this is a handbook on anti-marketing, where everything is contentious and where argument follows argument in a melange of non-sequiturs and repetitions.

Getting potential customers to go to your site, look at your cloud, read your billboard, play your game and stay enthralled for more than a few seconds is a completely different story. And then getting them to get their plastic out, is entering the realms of fantasy.

So, let's take a quick peep at the way we sell. Then and now

This is the sharp end of the marketing process. Life in the trenches. Up to our eyes in muck, exaggerations, partial and half-truths... and little white lies. In the past, it was easy. Well, easier, as has been previously said.

Just one basic rule: Kill. Kill. Kill. Get the sale, at all costs. Always Be Closing. It was a world where every customer/punter was simply measured by cash potential. If you were a sales person, who drove a Cadillac Eldorado then you were successful, but if you sympathised with the little old lady, who was confused and did not know what to do, then you were a failure. And quickly fired. On skid row. There was no room for being nice in this world. It was no wonder that 'The Art of War', by Sun Tsu, became one of the most quoted tests in traditional marketing. That was the only way to sell.

The foot soldiers of sales trudged the streets, banged on doors and grinned desperately at bored housewives. *'The jungle is dark, but full of diamonds,'* as Pinter evocatively put it in *'Death of a Salesman'*. Sales was a forbidding place, but if you could walk-the-walk and talk-the-talk, had a hide as tough as a rhino, then the diamonds would be tantalisingly within reach.

Postmodernism rarely got a look in with traditional marketing back then. There are a few notable exceptions. Take the brilliant original movie, *'Miracle on 34th Street'* - and the owner of Macy's department store suddenly proclaiming that theirs was going to be the store that told the truth, even if it meant sending customers to competitors. They would be known as the 'friendly' store. And all because the Santa guy in the store decided to be honest and refer people down the road, if customers could not find want they wanted in Macy's.

What about today? Selling in the 21st century - an age so complicated and chocful with instant information and stuffed with all sorts of cunning marketing campaigns, that most of us do not know which way to turn. Where does the sales person fit in?

For starters, no one really knows. There is no clear right and wrong way on how to do this sales thing. No black or white method. It is not just a matter of getting out there and using all your powers of persuasion. It has become a lot more psychological. You have to be sacred, ethical, green, principled, trust-based, sticky, reversed and very lateral to get to the big bucks. Why? Because the new age sales person needs to be liked. To be loved. Appreciated. Trusted. Accepted. Sales has become a nice job for nice people, who genuinely want to help others. Sales people have become Samaritans in suits.

This is very confusing to the traditional sales person, who has been brought up on a diet of Boston Matrices, PESTLE, ABC, AIDA and target-related bonuses.

Even today, most sales courses do not teach you how to be nice, gentle and sympathetic to the customer's needs. They do not teach you the value of walking away from deal, just because you want to. They do not teach you how to sacrifice your queen in order to win the game. They do not spend a lot of time on the psychology of the sales process and how to react to the customer's paranoias with cool, calm, assuredness and an almost carefree dismissiveness to the sale. There is still the steely vein of 'getting the sale' at the core of nearly all current sales manuals. No one spends too much time on the value of refusing or turning the sale down – in effect, throwing the fish back when you have caught it!

And even when this new type of selling is explained to the sales teams of today, it is generally met with looks of puzzlement and derision. It is as if they are being exposed to some type of novel sales suicide.

Cynics will say that such a lateral way of doing the sales thing could just be another crazy fad. Just another fancy way of getting the customer's money - but in a much more cunning and acceptably painless way.

The touchy-feely, customer-coddling, way of doing business might be just such a thing, but in the world of the Internet, businesses would be well advised to incorporate at least some of these new ways into their selling. It is a foolhardy marketing person indeed who ignores the power of the customer's feelings and moods.

The sales game has reached a new stage in its evolution, where understanding and assimilation of the customer's needs and wants are dominating the whole process and where money can be just an embarrassing bye-product of the sales game.

An excellent company (Home Language International) I used to work for a few years ago recently produced their new brochure for learning a language in the teacher's home. Now, in the past, they have always adopted the traditional way of getting business – Kotler-inspired adherence to the 'P's and the world revolving around targets, the marketing mix and the customer being king or queen. Imagine my surprise when I saw their new brochure and their strapline for the 'twenties'. It looks so out of place on the front cover of a sales brochure and yet it is so wonderfully warm, for lack of a better word.

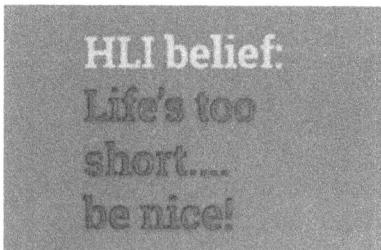

HLI belief:
Life's too
short....
be nice!

The Touchy-Feely Way

I went to a talk recently by David Tovey, a believer in something called 'principled selling'. He started by giving me a copy of his book (not surprisingly, called: *'Principled Selling', 2012*) for knowing the name of the first ever James Bond film. I cannot remember the exact context and did not have the heart to tell him that I already had a copy of his book (the reason for my attending his talk in the first place). But I was pleased to have sounded incredibly intelligent by saying 'Casino Royale' with David Niven and Peter Sellars - and not 'Dr No' and Sean Connery.

So, I was warmly smug as Tovey got stuck into his hour on principled selling. And my warmth grew, as I listened in increasing awe to this rather clever, well thought through take on it all. It was like taking that manager of Macy's at his word and creating a whole new philosophy around it.

Principled Selling

Basically, principled selling is an attempt to address the whole issue of using motivation not manipulation; of investing in profitable and long-term relationships; having the customer actively involved in the business development process and, most of all, being human, honest, polite and nice.

The buzz words are still there (Target–Motivate-Secure-Develop), but are softened by a realisation that the customer is a person to be treated more as a business 'friend', not just as a sack of cash. And there is a lot of talk about loyalty, networking, truth and giving value. Most of all, and more contentiously, the new era 'principled' sales team are encouraged to:

Give value	Be interesting
Be focused	Be polite
Be totally honest	Be generous
Be human	Be nice

This is a far cry from a 'traditional sales person - particularly the honesty bit. The 'always-be-closing' mantra is a distant memory when faced with having to be polite, human, generous and exuding empathy.

The principled selling 'ethic' goes further. Be persistent but never chase; recognise that your prospect controls the 'timing' of the sale; don't be afraid to walk from a sale and listen more than speak.

Obviously, we are talking of perfect marketing conditions here and not when the company is looking down the barrel, thinking seriously about redundancies and devoid of inspiration. Nevertheless, this is all a breath of fresh air to the postmodern sales person.

The sales person is no longer the villain or closet thief - this is far more the nice guy, who genuinely wants to help the customer through the entire sales process. The icing on the cake comes with advice like this: never make calls when you are in a bad mood; never use a script and always make friends with the 'gatekeeper' (receptionist / PA) when calling a new company or person.

We are now up to our ankles in postmodern, anti-selling - an area which most businesses are too frightened to jump into even nowadays. It is far easier to use scripts, sound bored and trundle through a ton of useless cold contacts every day, because that is the only way traditional sales people know how to sell.

Let's wade in a little deeper

And a strange case of serendipity too. David Tovey may have popularised this thing called principled selling, but in America, Tammy and Don Cardenas produced a slim volume along the same lines and with exactly the same title. It ventured to take the whole customer 'experience' thing a step further.

The whole process should, according to the Cardenases, just be about disseminating information - not even attempting to sell stuff to people who do not want it. It is about giving the customers what they need and want; staying in touch after the 'deal'; helping the customer make the right decision and… never lying, distorting or being selective with the truth. It is about being far more responsive to actual customer needs and then reacting caringly.

It could be argued that selling has now reached a new phase where being extra nice to the customer really is the vital component to the sale. Why? Because the repercussions of not being nice are too horrible to contemplate. The public can be a merciless lot, if it feels tricked or cheated and will exact revenge by using the apocalyptic 'one-star' rating, attached to a scathing review.

Thinking cynically for a change, it could be argued that sales and marketing people of today live in the shadow fear and horror of upsetting the customer, mainly because of the power of the Internet. We could claim that the modern age has created a more caring sales and marketing person, but that would be stretching it a bit. The leopard only changes its spots if nature has made it impossible to catch prey in the old way anymore. Spots are out. Stripes are in.

Today's marketing and sales person has to approach the whole hoary area of sales with tact, care, complete openness, a sense of humour, charm, and even friendliness … or the public will walk, no matter how much the sales person smiles and pleads with hand on heart and begging on bended knees.

In fact, they will walk much faster if there is any begging or pleading with hands, hearts and knees.

18. sacks of glitter

What about other ways of using anti-marketing and selling?

Ways of adapting postmodernist theory to the street. Enter the anti-marketing sales person with his/her array of sparkling tools in colourful toolboxes, intent on using a bit of magic and sacks of anti-glitter. So, let's flip open a few of these toolboxes and have a look at the stuff available to the postmodern marketing and sales person.

Reverse-Psychology Selling

This is probably one of the easiest to explain and yet one of hardest for a marketing or sales person to pull off successfully. Telling everyone that the product is not very good (which is the essence of reverse-psychology marketing), is a dangerous game to play at the best of times. Some brands however, manage this with considerable aplomb. Marmite use their '*you either love Marmite or hate it*' campaign, very slickly. By acknowledging that a vast proportion of the population really dislike their yeast product, they face their detractors head-on and actually use the negativity as a positive attribute.

Guinness pulled off a tongue-in-cheek masterstroke during the rugby world cup in Japan. They produced a brilliant two-day online campaign which attacked their own brand to the very core. Guinness is associated with the colour black so, after New Zealand (the All Blacks) had defeated Ireland in the competition, they produced a slick advertisement, which not only attacked themselves, but also encouraged their drinkers to have a day drinking Carlsberg – their main competitor and branded in Irish green, instead. The online 'poster' went viral within minutes with nearly 20,000 tweets and retweets – all with favourable comments. The strapline read: *'Have a pint of Carlsberg. We're officially done with the colour black today.'*

And the Yorkie chocolate biscuit people had a staggeringly-successful campaign, when they deliberately promoted their chocolate bar as the chosen confectionary for every macho, long-distance, truck driver. Posters and television commercials starred men with huge muscles biting off hunks of the bar, while driving massive 24-wheelers. The Yorkie marketing team then took things a step further and into very dangerous waters indeed, by putting a large *'Not For Girls'* warning on the wrapper. There was predictable outrage and… lots of free media coverage. But did it harm business? Of course not. It created a 'buzz' and lots of attention - which was excellent news for the marketing team. Plus, women and girls bought the bar as a protest at being 'banned'. Yorkie sales went through the roof.

Reverse-psychology marketing is doing the exact opposite to what any sane person would advise. Basically, it is tearing up the rule book and committing marketing suicide. But it should always be remembered, emphasised and repeated that the customer is a very strange creature, which always reacts unpredictably… predictably. Saying that your target market should not buy your product in a variety of novel ways seems daft from the outset. But people like to be treated as intelligent beings. They like a good joke, especially if it is self-inflicted.

In fact, the more you run your own stuff down or push business away, the more it attracts the postmodern customer. A baffled and chuckling public will be intrigued by these tactics and you will have them hooked, at least for a few more moments than if you had just shouted how great your things were.

Of course, this risky strategy does not work all the time. Gerald Ratner, the owner of a string of High Street jewellery shops, famously went on television and proclaimed that all his jewellery was cheap and nasty. He thought the public would laugh at such brazen cockiness and continue to buy his jewellery. They did not… and his business nearly went bankrupt.

Reverse-psychology marketing is great fun, because it plays with the dark side of marketing in a very cavalier manner. It is 'pleasure derived from pain' with large slabs of contradiction and masochism thrown in. It takes courage, gall, panache and considerable amounts of self-belief to pull it off. When it works, people remember the campaign, with a smile. When it fails, people also remember it with a smile, but for entirely different reasons.

Relationship and Engagement Marketing

Relationship marketing concentrates entirely on maintaining excellent relations with current customers. The principle goal is to retain custom by offering exemplary service. It is not so concerned with looking for new customers – the idea here being that word-of-mouth recommendation will naturally increase customer footfall. It also relies on a much more analytical approach with regular emails, mailshots and newsletters maintaining focus on the brand and product.

The problem nowadays is that relationship marketing has had to evolve into something else, something a little more 'human'. The most compelling reason for this is the recent change in the law over customer privacy and data protection. Businesses can no longer bombard clients with their love. The law now requires customers to be the active component, by agreeing to receive regular updates. This is a tricky situation since the majority of people will not agree to tick the box which allows more 'spam' into their lives, no matter how happy they are with a product.

And so, businesses are moving towards 'customer engagement' rather than continuing with 'customer relationship' building. The way they do this is not to concentrate on the selling of the product anymore, but on the selling of the services around the product. Customers are now being offered a better 'experience' rather than a better product. So, businesses are constantly thinking up ways of keeping the customer involved in the sales process. Websites have customer feedback pages and invitations to take part in product surveys. Customer comments and star ratings are vital. The customer has become an integral part of the whole sales process.

And the product is no longer centre stage.

Peripheral services have assumed increasing importance with speed, home delivery, instant availability and even the inclusion of the customer in the 'creation' of the product. For example, IKEA encourages potential customers to 'build' their own kitchens and bathrooms on IKEA customer computers at their superstores. The customer lays down the specifications and the store provides the materials in flat-pack boxes. The rest is up to the customer and a set of alum keys. IKEA sees the customer as the vital component at the start of the sales process and not just the end of the thing.

Airlines nowadays sell their seats not purely on price, although that is still important, of course. They distinguish themselves from competitors by emphasising extra legroom, faster check-ins, good food, quiet lounges and larger baggage allowances. It is the experience of the trip which sells the seats today, rather than just the price.

In fact, it could be argued that the really cheap airlines are suffering now because the 21st century passenger wants a better experience and not just a dirt cheap ticket and an hour of squashed, foodless misery, before starting a business trip or holiday.

The example of the Apple iPhone is another case of a relationship being created and maintained not just by the product itself. Customers are encouraged to 'revere' the box that the iPhone comes in, along with the various accessories - and even Apple stickers. Apple often boasts that the box is rarely thrown away by customers, because it is such a unique, pleasing design. The box has become a selling feature. People love the box, even though it has virtually no other practical use. It is almost a status symbol to have it on your desk.

Relationship marketing has switched to 'Engagement Marketing' as people want more than just the product, whether it is the free extras, the add-ons, being an active component in the product's design or just the nice packaging... and they will pay for it, because it makes them feel unique, special, interested, surprised, part of the seller's community and exclusive.

Marketing teams now consider the customer as part of their sales team, who is not just viewed as future cash potential, but more as a fundamental part in product development, appraisal and overall brand satisfaction. Total engagement has replaced a simple, one-way relationship.

Minimalist Marketing

In the 80s and 90s it was really 'cool' to walk around in a Lacoste / Polo / Adidas / Fred Perry shirt, along with similarly 'logo-ed' big brand jeans and trainers. People became walking billboards. As we reached the

21st century, some businesses (and people) reacted against this trend. Companies took the radical step of removing all visible branding and logos from their products or decided just to have a very small, discreet logo on a breast pocket or sleeve.

The reasoning here was that everyone should be their own brand and not just the sum total of all the major global clothing brands thrown together. Human individuality emerged. People bought clothing because of the colour and design which suited them and not because it was a 'trending' brand to wear.

Or did they? Marketing people are not so short-sighted.

Take Kanye West, the American rapper. He has a t-shirt clothing range, which is nothing different in style, quality or texture to other cheaper brands. The colours are plain too, with no motifs or special design features. But the product is unimportant. This is because it has a (hidden) Kanye West label on the collar... and crucially, retails at over 40 dollars a shirt, as opposed to 10 dollars for 'inferior' brands. Hugo Boss, Versace and Calvin Klein have all followed suit. Today, there is a vast array of no-logo clothing available, particularly online, without visible branding.

Customers are led to believe that only the really expensive brands have no visible labels! Nothing visible has become the new sophisticated, luxurious... and expensive. It is alluring, clandestine and selective. No logo has become synonymous with luxury and high-end brands.

Outside the clothing market, you only need to look at the restaurant industry. A few years back, notably in New York, Tokyo and London, a series of independent restaurants started popping up with no name or no visible logos on the exterior fascia of their buildings. There was nothing to indicate that inside was a fantastic place to eat. These restaurants subsequently made their name purely by word-of-mouth recommendation - and actively shunned big marketing or a catchy name, to drag hungry punters in. They became 'secret' eating clubs, where only a select few dined. Not only did this increase customer satisfaction and the whole eating experience, but also created a new type of fierce loyalty. People love to be treated as special.

And so, the no-brand logo has become a brand in itself, with one American restaurant actually taking the whole thing to the bizarre extreme by naming their place - *'The Bar With no Name'*. Not only did this emphasis the coolness of the no-logo image, but also hearkened back to the classic Clint Eastwood westerns of old, which starred *'the man with no name'*. When Clint breezed into town, everyone sat up and took notice, despite not knowing who he was or where he came from. His guns did the talking and word-of-mouth did the rest. The man-with-no-name brand spawned at least five subsequent movies! A lovely example of minimalist / retro / hyper-reality.

If you want to get a better idea on the power of branding, then look no further than Naomi Klein's book, *'No Logo' (1999)*. It is a frightening account of 'big brand' marketing, where *'the brand is not a reflection of quality, but a reflection of what the marketing department wants it to stand for.'*

Storytelling

Storytelling has been around since time immemorial and has been used by marketing teams as the bedrock of many successful campaigns. But what puts it into the postmodern, anti-marketing top ten, is the fact that numbers and statistics are irrelevant.

People believe stories because they are compelling, interesting and very human. They do not appeal to logic or reason. From the dawn of time, people have told stories. It is one of the principle reasons why human beings are different from animals and is fundamental to how we have developed over time.

In marketing, it is a perfect tool to get our messages across. The classic storytelling advertisement of all time in the UK was the 80s *'Gold Blend'* romance saga. This was a story that customers happily bought into and wanted to believe. A ridiculous romance between a pair of flirting business people over a series of 30-second television commercials, over cups of steaming coffee. It was the 'will-they-won't-they' aspect, which had viewers hooked. Gold Blend even did pre-advertisements, designed to inform the public when the next episode would hit the screen (a delicious example of self-referential daftness). Gold Blend coffee sold by the lorry-load, of course, and no house was complete without a jar in the cupboard! The storyline of the Gold Blend couple still lingers as a prime example of storytelling at its most effective in a marketing setting. It was reality TV / soap / romance / titillation and selling all at the same time.

Nowadays, storytelling is very much part and parcel of the marketing game. Recently, it has been taken to startling lengths with marketing people actually making full-length movies to advertise their products. The Catalonian lager, *'Estrella Dam'* produced a well-plotted, dramatic movie with 'A-list' actors to promote their lager. Estrella Dam lager was placed in pretty-much every scene and yet... the whole film still worked as a cool and trendy cultural reflection of beach life in Spain. Turkish Airlines have followed suit with a similar epic with the renowned director, Ridley Scott, behind the camera.

Storytelling is a human way of getting not just the message across, but in getting the message to 'stick' in the memory of the viewer. Stories appeal to the emotions, the senses, to our innermost feelings and are the best way of explaining things which would be forgotten very quickly, if told in a factual and rather dry manner.

Professor Stephen Brown of Ulster University wrote a book called *'Postmodern Marketing'* in the 90s. It was a great work of theory and thoroughly readable and yet... such works of wisdom are, by their very nature, a hard hill to climb. Then he wrote a series of three novels, beginning with *'The Marketing Code'* (a loose pastiche / parody of Dan Brown's *'The Da Vinci Code'*), which discussed the broader issues of postmodernist marketing, but woven into the framework of a thumpingly-good and very funny novel. Anyone who has read this book will instantly recall scenes involving *'Quantum Marketing'*, *'Three-Times-a-Lady Marketing'* and the insanely-funny Acronym Department. This is storytelling of the finest nature and gets a difficult message across almost as a bye-product of the main plot.

Basically, brands are stories. Brown says (*'Brands and Branding',* 2016) that we do not experience the world through information. We experience it through a story.

Dark Marketing

Keeping with Professor Stephen Brown, we move into the shady areas of dark marketing. He explains this marketing variation in his brilliant book, *'Brands and Branding'* (2016). This is the murky area of 'dirty tricks' or 'bad-taste' marketing. Dirty tricks speaks for itself: denigrating the competition, being 'sneaky' or even using physical violence to destroy the competition.

Just one example - a sneaky one. Outlets in airport departure terminals always request passenger boarding cards at the point of purchase. Apparently, I am reliably told, this has nothing to do with security - it is purely an exercise in amassing marketing data. But people never even think of questioning this, because airports are such security-conscious environments, where to say the wrong word or just to 'look suspicious' can get you into very hot water. Sneaky indeed.

As regards denigrating the competition, well, saying that Hugo Boss made SS uniforms in the last war,

Colonel Sanders was convicted of manslaughter, or that Coco Chanel spied for the Nazis, might be seen as deliberately attempting to damage their brands.

Stephen Brown categorizes dark marketing into 5 scurrilously mean areas, beginning with 'Light Dark' and ending with 'Fright Dark'. It is a worryingly humorous breakdown.

For example, Light Dark might be naming your restaurant Fawlty Towers and then deliberately giving appalling service, whilst at the other end of the extreme, Fright Dark might cover websites selling illegal drugs, child pornography or promoting race or cultural hatred in all its worst forms.

This is the area of marketing (notably on the Internet), which starts with reverse-psychology and parody… and ends perilously treading the line between the marginally-legal and the extremely illegal.

Two final and intriguing examples of dark marketing, are what the UK Advertising Standards Authority (ASA) label 'gender-stereotyping'. These might slip into the 'Slightly-Light-Dark' category, depending on your predilections towards sexism.

The first was a television commercial which went like this: two men are so overcome by the deliciousness of Philadelphia Cheese, that they forget that they have put their respective babies onto a moving food conveyor-belt (much like the ones used in the restaurant chain, *'Yo Sushi'*). It was supposed to be a humorous take on the powers of Philadelphia Cheese, but after nearly 200 people complained to the ASA about the suggestion that 'men are incapable of caring for children', the advertisement was withdrawn.

Similar complaints were lodged to the ASA about a Volkswagen commercial, which depicted men engaged in adventurous activities like mountaineering, while women sat on park benches, looking bored with baby buggies beside them. More complaints for fairly obvious reasons.

Dark marketing teeters on the brink of being offensive to someone. It can seem relatively harmless to most people, but in today's society, it is a brave (or foolhardy) marketeer indeed that does not assess all potential campaigns from all points of view before embarking on something that could be extremely costly in both money and prestige, as well as damaging to the brand itself. It also covers marketing that deliberately goes right over the edge in all its most hurtful ways.

Accidental Marketing

Accidental marketing is not the result of marketing strategy, but just the result of some random event. The classic example involved Chanel No.5 - the perfume. Legend has it that many years ago, sales were flagging slightly… that is until Marilyn Monroe was asked by a slightly intrusive reporter what she wore in bed at night. She replied: *"Just a dab of Chanel No.5 behind each ear."* You can imagine what happened to sales the next day.

Then there is the story of 'Mentos', the minty US sweet. Again, sales were pootling along, but then some kid experimented in his garage with a tub of Mentos and a vat of cola. The resultant chemical reaction was an instant hit on YouTube and rapidly went viral. Next day, Mentos sold out across the US, as kids attempted to replicate the experiment. The strange thing here was that the marketeers of Mentos had no idea what was happening. After all, they were selling a minty sweet, not a frothy bomb!

Accidental marketing is not all peaches and cream. It can backfire spectacularly. A popular pub chain in the middle of the UK tried a new children's menu a few years ago, with a 'horsey' theme. Timing is everything in marketing and this campaign came out just days before a horse-meat scandal hit many supermarkets across the UK. To try promoting a *'Super Horse Kids Burger'* at such a moment was not at all advisable and the campaign was ditched almost before it began.

Shock Marketing (Shockvertising)

Shockvertising is another example of marketing people appealing to the raw emotions of an easily-offended public. And shock, by its nature, is always meant to be dramatic and controversial. Back in the early 90s, the large Italian clothing manufacturer, Benetton, produced a series of posters for billboards, which were at the extreme edge of advertising. The Benetton baby (a new-born baby in all its 'gore') was banned as being 'offensive to public sensibility' by the UK Advertising Standards Authority, whilst, at the same time, it won a prize from the Swiss General Poster Association. It clearly divided opinion, but crucially… created a stir.

Benetton enthusiastically followed this up with more posters along similar lines. Barrack Obama photoshopped into a picture kissing the Chinese premier. Stark pictures of HIV sufferers, guerrilla fighters in Africa and finally three human hearts labelled black, white and yellow, pushed the campaign into very controversial waters indeed. The product has become secondary to the message, which was designed to tweak human conscience and make a make a brutal, moral comment on an issue of the times.

In the English language industry, Berlitz language schools used this technique in the 90s to great effect, with a campaign depicting scenes which needed local language knowledge for vital information. For example, one poster showed a vast, deserted beach with a warning sign in Farsi, which implied that going onto the beach might not be a good idea. But we do not know why. Only Farsi readers of the sign knew the secret. So... the implicit message was - go to Berlitz and learn Farsi!

Another poster depicted a bizarre and rather aggressive looking alien waving its tendrils at you, with the caption: *'The most dangerous creature in the universe. As long as you speak to him in Chinese, everything is OK.'*

Shockvertising can be humorous, as in the Berlitz examples. Indeed, Berlitz has used the same tongue-in-cheek marketing in their television commercials (e.g. the German coastguard's radio conversation with the captain of a ship in distress and the confusion over the words - sinking and thinking).

Sky have used this method as well. The campaign to highlight the new Sky Arts channel used posters depicting guitars and amplifiers, next to a caption saying: *'Loud, obnoxious and infantile.'*

Shockvertising is a way of startling the viewer and creating controversy. If the campaign is mentioned by the media or banned in any way, then... job done.

Ethical Marketing

Ethical Marketing stands tall in postmodernist marketing as a true signpost for the future. It is very much a product of the 'new' honesty that the Internet has initiated and relies on 'green' issues and social responsibility.

It stems from the simple belief that behaviour defines the brand more than marketing and that ethical products might command a slightly higher price (e.g. Fairtrade coffee, organic vegetables etc.), but will leave the planet in a better and healthier condition.

Even big corporations are trying to hitch their wagon to the ethical train, for obvious reasons. To be seen as attempting to reverse global warming or deforestation is good for the brand. It shows that big businesses care. And (thinking a tad, cynically) caring in the 21st century is good for sales. This is a care which stretches from the macro to the micro, from planetary issues to care of our own country and our own individual health.

It is also why supermarkets have suddenly started expounding the virtues of all sorts of healthy foodstuffs like carrots, pomegranates and blueberries over red meat, alcohol and high calorific food. They believe it is good to be seen to be caring for our health and not just their profits. To be ethical is to show that there is a greater understanding of the moral duty to the customer.

Shell and BP have new flower logos, while McDonalds are now selling salads. Micro-breweries are also enjoying a new popularity as they promote their beer range, which is made in the 'old' ways without chemicals and preservatives.

The only problem is that customers tend to view green products as being more expensive than the mass-produced alternatives, particularly when it comes to food. The big conundrum here is that to be healthy and to save the planet is going to cost you a lot more than staying unhealthy and not bothering about the polar bear.

One way that marketeers found of addressing this issue is something called 'Wackaging'. This first example occurred in the early 'Noughties', when a drinks company called 'Innocent' began a novel campaign which involved their products 'talking' to potential customers by way of funny, clever, cutesy, quirky and inevitably... irritating messages on the packaging. Hence, wacky-packaging or 'wackaging'.

At first, it seemed a wonderful way of being persuasive in a friendly and 'jokesy' way. And the marketing slant here was that the product actually 'told' the customer about how it could improve his/her life, without being overtly-aggressive or condescending.

Messages like: *'keep me in the fridge'*, *'wash me thoroughly'* and somewhat obviously, *'please eat me soon'*, started springing up on products from bananas to energy drinks. Then the messaging added pithy humour to the mix (*'open other end'* or *'I like it more in the cupboard'*), followed by simple 'educational' soundbites. A great example is the 'Innocent Smoothie' which gave dictionary definitions of the words: pernickety, finicky and punctilious on the label, along with the line: *'all these words are a fancy way of saying fussy. And we're experts on when it comes to fussy...'*

'Higgedy Pies' offered 'morale-boosting-dinners', while Tyrell's crisps claimed their 'sweet and salty' offering was a *'boon for the indecisive'*. Even Waitrose weighed in with the pithy packaging… on their herb range! You could buy a packet of *'Beautiful Bay Leaves',* which were described as *'the essential Bouquet Garni or Baccalaureate'*. The jury is still out as to what Waitrose was up to here… which might just be the point. Leave the customer wondering and in confusion, but crucially thinking about bay leaves on the way home afterwards.

The company, 'Rude Health', not only sold their almond, hazelnut or coconut milk as an 'organic' alternative, but also added cheeky little lines on the back of their products like: *'You're in rude health when you've pole-danced on a lamp-post, never taken a dive in a football game… or packed a skipping rope on a business trip'*.

Humour, health and silliness all neatly-packaged together and designed to show the customer that even businesses with serious ethical messages can be light-hearted and funny, as well as deflecting customers from thinking about the slightly higher price.

Sacred-selling

This is probably as far from traditional sales and marketing as you could possibly get. Sacred-selling bases itself on a very simple premise - that it offers real care and interest in potential customers, even if a sale is not achieved. It is one step further down the moral line than 'ethical' marketing.

Making money here is never the prime reason of selling – which might seem a total contradiction. It is far more about the 'joy' of serving without the heavy weight of sales targets and conversion rates hanging heavily around the sales person's shoulders.

The extremely admirable mantra of the scared seller is: *'You'll develop real relationships with people, who will gladly purchase what you are offering, because they like you. And even when they don't, you'll both feel good about the conversation.'*

The sacred sales person looks at sales as part of a process and not as an end in itself. It is a way of creating a harmony between sellers and buyers, where money is not the prime motivator of the trade.

Cold 'tele-sales' has forever been the sharp end of the sales process, but recently, forward-thinking companies have employed sacred-selling as a way of creating better relations and feedback from the customer. Badgering and hassling a potential customer with pre-written, intrusive, pressurized scripts, has been replaced with 'genuine' concern over the customer's well-being, along with free, uninitiated advice.

I recently had a call from a mobile phone operator in Delhi, who seemed more interested in my recent holiday in India and the food I had eaten there, than in selling me anything. At first, I was irritated by the interruption of the call, but I warmed to the person at the other end as the call developed. I felt much more inclined to buy the new Samsung Galaxy than ever before simply because this person did NOT sell it to me and seemed interested in me as a human being and not just a sales opportunity. He even ended the call by telling me that he himself preferred iPhones!

Of course, this all might be clever marketing tactic (and it probably was), but so what? It was a much better experience than being talked at for 30 seconds… and then having to press the disconnect button with a sour taste in my mouth.

Trust-Based Marketing

Trust-based marketing is exactly that. Rather than pursuing sales relentlessly and seeing clients as bags of money, TBM relies on building relationships and establishing total trust between the buyer and seller.

The basis of TBM is brand loyalty over the long term. In a way, it has moved quite far from what is perceived as 'push marketing' and into an era of 'pull-marketing', where potential customers are encouraged to be the active force. TBM places all information before the customer in an easy, friendly manner and lets him or her decide, without any pressure. But once TBM has you… it has you for life.

A simple personal example: I always buy 'Anadin Extra' as my preferred headache cure, rather than Boots' own or other brands, which are cheaper. Both contain identical ingredients, I am told, but I still buy the more expensive tablets. Why? Because I always have done, since I was a boy. There is no logical reason, except that I trust the 'Anadin' brand to cure my headaches over all others.

Similarly, I eat 'Weetabix' cereal for breakfast and shun other identical products. Same reason. I have always eaten Weetabix. I like the brand. I like the packet! I should also add that I have a strange feeling of loyalty to Weetabix, because the main Weetabix factory is in a place called Burton Latimer in Northamptonshire, just 10 minutes' drive from where I lived my entire childhood. So, it is more 'nostalgia' than total trust here – which is just another form of TBM!

TBM creates customer trust in a variety of interesting ways. First, if my dentist says a particular brand of toothpaste is the best, then I will go ahead and buy it, despite knowing deep-down that the dentist is probably getting free samples and perhaps a bonus from the manufacturer, though I have not worked out how. Trust is created here from the voice of authority. The same goes for a doctor's advice or even what a plumber, mechanic or builder would tell me about a problem I may have. They clearly know more about their own specialised area than I do. So, I trust them and go ahead and do what they say.

There are other areas which create total trust, like longevity. We trust a long-established company, rather than one which opened last week! We also trust businesses which are promoted by our heroes (e.g. sports people, TV personalities and actors), who put their faces to products and encourage their fans to trust the product too. We all know that the celebrity is getting some kick-back for this endorsement, but that never seems to matter, for lots of illogical reasons. We still all go out and buy the stuff.

Then, there is familiarity and frequency. If we are bombarded with TV commercials about a particular product we are, strangely enough, more inclined to trust it than a product which remains in the shadows of advertising. I think I would use the comparison site, 'Go Compare' over all others, simply because their advertisement is on my screens several times a night – every night. I know it is subliminal and I should not, but I trust the daft opera singer, for some inane reason I cannot work out. TBM is best described as:

- **Getting the customer's attention... then interest**
- **Establishing a certain familiarity**
- **Creating an illogical trust**
- **Forming a binding relationship which will last a very long time**

Agile Marketing

Agile marketing is a much more recent phenomenon, which combines some of the aspects of traditional marketing with anti-marketing techniques.

It is a highly-organised approach to the way that marketing statistics are analysed and interpreted and how it reacts to the chaos and unpredictability of customer buying habits. The concept has been borrowed from the way IT software businesses are set up.

Team morale is of paramount importance and workers are placed in positions which they are best-suited for and actually prefer. The concentration is on staff and processes, so that there is much less stress and anxiety.

Budgets are normally devolved to the individual level, so that small campaigns can be carried out by lower-level marketing and sales people - and everyone has unrestricted access to all available information. The idea here is to encourage creativity, self-belief, trust, respect and pride.

As far as the customer is concerned, he or she is included in the whole marketing process and drives all campaigns. Agile marketing rests on everything being extremely fluid, recognising that the customers' needs and desires are constantly changing and that all marketing plans should be likewise.

And the rest...

I could go on and on and on, listing more and more bizarre and extreme forms of marketing and selling, which have sprung up over the last few years and have their own gang of followers. I am not saying these approaches are wrong, or that they do not work. They all probably do... and do not. Marketing is like that. You can create your own piece of genius and immediately get it out there on the Internet. Suddenly, you have found yet another Holy Grail, which will take marketing into a new age, or make you a few pounds if you sell it as a paperback with a catchy title.

I could list stuff like: sticky marketing, stickier marketing, 'Purple Cow' marketing, herd marketing, evangelical marketing and my favourite, 'defensive pessimism', which is about as bleak as marketing can get, since it holds 'the power of negative thinking' as a positive resource in the marketing department.

What is universally agreed, is that in the 21st century there has to be far more emphasis on empathy, patience, trust, honesty, understanding and 'gentle' persistence. The customer has to be treated as a delicate, moody, easily-offended and illogical creature, which should be quietly coaxed into making a decision, which we will all respect and be happy with, even if it does not quite work out the way we intended.

It has become a far more psychological game with sales and marketing people having to think very laterally, constantly having to put themselves into their clients' shoes and then walking the extra mile feeling extremely uncomfortable and falling over lots of times.

SECTION NINE:

interlude –
a look back at
how it was

19. when I was a boy...

...the teacher asked the class what we all wanted to be when we grew up.

50 sticky hands went up and little voices shouted out loudly:

'pilot, spaceman, actor, ballerina, train driver, postman, builder, farmer, soldier, racing car driver, mechanic, artist, sailor, bank manager, lorry driver, robber, businessman or woman, balloonist, spy, secret agent, superhero, grocer, hairdresser, fashion designer, model, Olympic champion, footballer, zoo keeper, vet, doctor, nurse, bin-man, road sweeper...'

No one said sales or marketing person.

And yet, this is the one profession which surrounds children from the moment they are born. In shops, supermarkets, department stores - you name it, they are there at every turn. And all are nice, smiling and superficially friendly people, who look as though they have had one too many coffees that morning and have spent rather too long looking at themselves in the mirror with a comb or bag of make-up, before venturing out.

So why don't children all clamour to be sales and marketing people from the pram upwards? Particularly sales people. It seems like a great job. You only have to look happy, wear nice clothes and stay in the warmth all day long, talking. No heavy lifting or hours of mindless driving on dangerous roads. Nothing that difficult at all. Just smiling and talking.

Simple answer: because children are taught not to see sales or marketing people as positive role models. You can dream of robbing banks, chasing the robbers, driving fire engines, and even putting on a uniform and going to foreign countries to shoot other people. There is some honour in all of these 'professions'. Some glamour and dare I say... pride?

As for sales and marketing, I grew up thinking that the people in this profession were the lowest of the low. One step up from a fraudster, charlatan, hustler or plain trickster. Not to harp on about this, but my own early experiences as a boy showed how the sales and marketing person was vilified, attacked and lampooned at every opportunity.

My parents saw it as a 'grubby' profession, because it involved money (their money) and what they perceived as various levels of deceit. I watched from my buggy as they closed the front door on the many door-to-door salesmen without so much as a hello, goodbye or thank you.

Then I went to school and was introduced to Shakespeare. Ironically, one of the first plays we all read in class was 'The Winter's Tale', which contains a nice array of caricatures, including one which my English teacher, Mr Peters, particularly liked. Autolycus was the Tudor equivalent of the travelling salesman and spent his life duping peasants and country folk out of their hard-earned money – he also had a questionable attitude to the young, impressionable females he met. Mr Peters called him a rogue, scallywag, liar, cheat and generally not a very pleasant sort of fellow - and that he liked him... a lot. This confused little Adrian a bit.

Then we moved onto Chaucer. Don't forget that in my days, education meant a lot of learning, reading and thinking, writing and testing. Chaucer was just another stepping stone to a coveted 'O' Level grade 2. And so, the Pardoner reared his sinister head in *'The Canterbury Tales'*. Mr Peters liked him too. True, he was unscrupulous, devious, deceitful and the sort who would sell his own grandmother, but Mr Peters argued that his 'marks' got what they deserved, because they were either stupid or easily-duped. Mr Peters did not take prisoners. He believed that the only way to survive was to give the world a damn good thrashing as often as possible. Incidentally, his hobby was collecting whips, which he hung around his study. But that is another story...

I moved on through Willy Loman (Arthur Miller's *'Death of a Salesman'*), and a whole selection of sales and marketing people in literature. I then branched out on my own and read a little Terry Pratchett and met Cut-My-Own-Throat Dibbler' – another incarnation of Autolycus and the Pardoner. Pratchett does not attack this gent much – there is far too much humour to be milked from him. Dibbler became what is now termed 'a loveable rogue'. This was the ground occupied by television's Arthur Daley (*'Minder'*), Del Boy (*'Only Fools and Horses')* and Flash Harry (*'St. Trinian's'* films) – all important figures during my informative years!

I started to grow up and became an English language teacher. A teacher who watched Bernard Cribbins as the spoons salesman in *'Fawlty Towers'*. And we all know what happened to him at the end of that episode. I also dipped my toe into gutsy American dramas, which involved sales people. The Americans do not really go down the road occupied by the lovable rogue. In their dramas, television shows and films (sorry, movies) we get a very clear idea of how they want to portray sales and marketing people. Shows like 'Shark Tank', 'Ballers', 'House of Lies', 'Mad Men', 'The Profit' and even 'Suits' do not leave a very favourable impression of the person wanting to sell stuff. We are back to sell, sell, sell and kill, kill, kill again.

And finally, there is Kafka. Franz Kafka. There is always Kafka. Most English graduates come across Franz at some time or other in their ascent to literary understanding. The principle character of *'Metamorphosis'* is a certain unfortunate called Gregor Samsa. He wakes up one morning to find out that he has changed into a massive, repulsive insect. His occupation is, of course, travelling salesman - and now he really is a monstrous parasite.

So, as you can see, my own personal voyage through life has not been particularly sales-friendly. At best, sales and marketing people are to be laughed at and certainly not to be believed, trusted or taken seriously.

And so, we move gently towards the Internet generation...

Things have changed in today's world

With the advent of the customer-led Internet, we have all become sales and marketing people. Everyone. Suddenly, we have all been given the power to sell and market on a global scale. That is just the way it is. Life has changed. The monkeys have been given the keys to the banana plantation. And we have all become parasites, great and small.

The Internet has changed it all and with it, the traditional perception of the sales and marketing person has altered dramatically. People realise that there really is a role in society for these 'parasites', after all. It is like discovering that rats, wasps and cockroaches actually do have a role to play in the food chain and that, more worryingly, we all contain rat/wasp/cockroach DNA.

Suddenly, we all are experiencing how hard it is to sell and market in today's society and that perhaps there is some art/science/craft to the whole messy thing. People are now studying business and all aspects of marketing at universities and colleges in increasing numbers and with considerable gusto.

The Internet has shown us the door to a paradise of gold and untold wealth. It is up to us to look for the key and start appreciating the magic of marketing!

However, I am still not sure if parents today would be delighted if their 4-year-old proclaimed loudly one morning that he or she wanted to be a sales or marketing person when he or she grew up. Old habits die hard.

20. some old advice

Quite a few years later, while in Japan, I was inadvertently given the basic tools of postmodern selling, or what I now like to call anti-marketing. I did not know it then - I was far too young to understand the connotations of such a radical view of selling. Remember, those were the days when the sale was all that mattered and to hell with the customer.

It was a very likeable sales manager (a Mr Takaoka), who explained it all to me. He worked for the biggest steel company in the world at that time (Nippon Steel) and believed in something very different to the mainstream Japanese sales manager. It took a vat of Saki to unlock his secrets, but here they are, as I noted them afterwards.

1. **Listen more than you talk**
2. **Always focus on client's needs - not your own**
3. **Forget the money part**
4. **Respect (never interrupt)**
5. **Be respectful at all times**
6. **Never criticize the client in any way**
7. **Build trust (nod a lot and smile)**
8. **Tell a story (about anything)**
9. **Talk about golf**
10. **Be positive about your products**
11. **Be a little negative about your products**
12. **Be enthusiastic, but not too loud**
13. **Never appear desperate**
14. **Never smoke at the first meeting**
15. **Never criticize the competition**

16.   Be prepared to walk away
17.   Always be polite

At the time, I did not really understand any of the points, particularly the storytelling, the being negative and walking-away bits. They seemed symptomatic of a depressed sales person on a very bad day. Now, when I read this list, I realise that it encapsulates everything that the postmodern sales person is trying to achieve today, apart from the smoking and possibly, the golf bits. It also reminds me of a quotation from an unknown source, which was pinned on the office wall of a sales department I was lucky enough to work in, in the 90s

His thoughts were slow
His words were few
And never made to glisten
But he was a joy
Wherever he went
You should have heard him listen

So, there you have it

Practical postmodernist anti-marketing, in a nut-shell. I could go on… and most definitely, will. But before I get back to the nip and tuck of being 'nice' while marketing or selling, I want to return to my own field of war – the English language industry. Why? Because I want to demonstrate how things can change in very practical marketing terms, almost overnight, from the traditional to the postmodern.

So, here is how it happened in the English language industry. This is another story – a slightly longer one. And a nicer one - a very anti-marketing one with a warm, cuddly ending. Enjoy…

21.teddy bear wars

Once upon a time…

…not so long ago, men and women in my industry travelled the world with heavy cases jam-packed with brochures, posters, video cassettes and, if you were lucky, USB memory sticks. These were the tools of the trade. The weapons in our armoury. We went to see travel agents, specialist language travel agents and attended countless public fairs in large, noisy halls from Buenos Aires to Bangkok and San Francisco to Seoul. It was a busy, tiring time, where you learnt the subway systems of each big city and survived on anything that a passing Starbuck's could throw at you.

All was fine and dandy in this strange world. Sales people explained their English courses to bewildered foreign agents and swore on their grandmother's life that the sun always shone brightly out of a blue sky in the UK.

We also claimed that all our host families consisted of two loving parents called Smith, a polite, snub-nosed boy, a beautiful blonde-haired girl and a nice, friendly golden Labrador, always called Sebastian). And these families lived in semi-detached houses in safe neighbourhoods, close to stations or bus stops, with Hugh Grants and Julia Roberts' as their neighbours. And Japanese, Brazilian, Korean, Chinese, Russian, Argentinian and European students all believed it…

… and came to our little island in their droves. Adults of all ages and, in the summer, herds of small children, out for an adventure language holiday in magnificent historic locations such as Clacton-on-Sea, Reading, Kettering and Swindon.

Then it all changed, because it had to.

There was no real distinction anymore in the industry. Schools, by their nature, were just schools and classes were taught in the same way across the country by teachers with the same qualifications and training. We did try to sell the gourmet nature of our cafés, the number or toilets per floor and the huge range of nationalities attending our courses - from Mongolian to Surinamese!   But we were running out of inspiration.   Agents and students had heard it all before and were becoming bored and turning their attention to newer, safer, sun-soaked destinations like Australia, New Zealand… and Malta.   Bookings began to dwindle in UK schools.

All seemed lost and schools started to close down. Teachers were leaving the industry and getting jobs as long-distance truck drivers, shop assistants or trainee baristas in coffee outlets. It was getting seriously bad.

Then… at the crucial moment, when the industry teetered on the edge of oblivion, something happened. It was like that moment when Clint rides into a Wild West town besieged by bandits, or when Frodo discovers the 'One Ring', or when Bruce Willis leans out of a window 100 floors up and invites everyone to party. It was that sort of moment.

Along came a man called Trevor. And he had an idea.

It was an idea so startling, so brilliant, so different and so clever, that it would change the industry forever.

Trevor represented a great little school situated in the lovely city of Exeter in the south-west of England - a safe, leafy, typically-English town. Business was on the downturn there too, so Trevor decided to do something about it.

He decided, on a whim, to jettison all his brochures, posters and literature, just before a long marketing trip to Japan. He simply left them behind in a large pile by his desk. He then did something quite extraordinary. Something that was possibly the first tangible example of extreme postmodernism or anti-marketing in a tired, stuffy and very traditional industry.

He packed his now empty case with about two hundred small, plush, teddy bears, each sporting a nice little sash, upon which was written the name of his school. And that was that.

No glossy literature, no long explanations of his English courses and no inane descriptions of fictitious host families. He then got on a plane to Tokyo. Legend has it that the whole city was soon alive with Exeter bears. They were on desks, tables, by front doors, next to pot-plants and on every windowsill. His cute little army was everywhere. And they were universally adored by counsellors and potential students alike, because the Japanese love cute and fluffy things. It is in their nature.

And so, naturally, everyone wanted to go to his school. After all, it was the home of the cutest, most 'ka-wa-ii' (that's Japanese for cute) bear in the world.

Trevor had found a truly original USP. It defied convention, broke the rules, was extremely anti-academic and was devastatingly successful.

He had a bear. The bear. And no one else did.

Bookings soared.

But others were listening.

They had noticed the bear invasion. Of course, they had. This was marketing and sales. The competition had its ears pricked. Hastily-convened meetings were called in basements across the western world with just one item on the agenda – the bear.

Suddenly, academic prowess, great teachers, magnificent toilets, 'cordon-bleu' fish and chips, the loveliest host families on the planet and the 'bestest', most amazingly-excellent exam results, meant nothing. What mattered most was the bear. Nothing but the bear. Because the bear spelt success. And success spelt money.

Schools started designing their own bears and rolling them out by the thousand. Big ones, small ones, tiny ones, furry ones, extra-furry ones, gold, red, blue, brown and black ones. Bears by the division, by the army, were soon ready for action, all armed with small, silk sashes and winning smiles.

And so, teddy bear wars began.

Schools sent their ursine armies to the four corners of the world, intent on ousting the Exeter ursine empire. Agents' desks were rapidly covered in bears not just from England, but from Australia, New Zealand, Ireland and eventually America (which were the biggest bears, of course). Offices started to resemble toy shops.

And then the serious stuff started.

Sales people started 'bearnapping' competitors' bears when counsellors were not looking, during meetings. Bears were pushed into nearby bins or kicked under dusty tables. It was a dark moment in an industry which normally prided itself on fair play in the field of battle. It was also not a particularly good time for teddy bears.

And so, we reached the turning point in the English language industry. It was now not important to sell courses, schools, accommodation and host families. Even price and commission did not matter. What was of prime importance was the cuteness of the bear and the deviousness of the sales person to have the last bear standing.

The war then became more metaphysical, more psychological. Schools began to compete with one another in terms of quality and plushness, trying to prove that the best-looking bear reflected the quality of the school. Schools like 'International House' made extra fluffy, golden-furred ones, the 'Hampstead

School of English' produced bears with individual characters. A school called 'Malvern House' produced tiny, jointed, furless creations, which looked a bit cheap… and sales dived, catastrophically.

A fluffy bear with plush, soft, fur, beady eyes and a quizzical expression was good for sales – it made the school look well-cared for, friendly and probably where a student would learn English in a cuddly environment. A cheaply-produced ursine creation probably reflected what the school was like… and the quality of the teachers.

It became most unsavoury. Bears with nice fur sold courses. Bears which refused to sit up properly on desks and fell over all the time, did not.

And then things evolved again.

It was indeed a time of shifting sands in the English language industry. Bears metamorphosed into fluffy cats, dragons, doggies and all manner of toys. Anything fluffy would do – as long as it was cute and promoted the school (via plush and sash) to wide-eyed agents and students.

Trevor had altered the fundamental fabric of marketing time and space in the English language industry. Suddenly, the product or price were no longer the most important things. Neither were any of the other Ps. Ps were redundant, useless. Unless one of them stood for Plush. As for the marketing mix – in the bin as well! Trevor had proved that the 'Speed-of-Fluff' out-performed everything else.

The industry took a deep breath as we reached the end of the millennium. It tried to take stock. This was indeed the dawn of a new and worrying age. Image had become the all-important factor and meant everything. Not the school or the teachers, but the image. And nothing sold the new image better than superior fluff. The bear was the school. The bear was the brand. Simple as that.

Anti-marketing had arrived in the English language world. Low culture selling high culture, if you like. Hyper-reality in the form of a toy bear doing a much better job than a sales person. A stuffed toy worth far more than a hatful of awards or points of excellence. The bear was gold dust.

Arguably, the best bears in the industry were produced by the *Hampstead School of English*. Excellent quality, intelligent-looking, happy, friendly, easy-to-carry and all with individual characters and expressions. A true reflection of the school at that time.

And we all lived happily ever after…

The industry had progressed from 'The Stone Age' of traditional marketing, through 'The Bronze Age' of modernist marketing (i.e. selling toilet facilities and school cafes) to 'The Cute Age' (anti-marketing), where the tools were fluffy and cuddly.

We move to the present day.

It has all become a lot more sophisticated now, of course. It could be argued that we are now living in the 'Cyber-Cute Age', where emojis, emotikons and all manner of digital 'fluff', gets peddled to potential customers. But that might be stretching the point a little too much.

So... what of its creator - the man who had proved that cute was indeed the 'dark matter' of modern-day marketing in the English language industry? What happened to him?

Legend has it that Trevor disappeared one day from the industry and has never been seen again. Some say he is out there somewhere developing the next stage in English language marketing, whilst others say he has a secret training school on an island somewhere in the Caribbean. Still more claim that he now lives in the south-west of England and is writing extremely successful, pornographic novels.

I doff my hat to him – an anti-marketing Jedi knight way ahead of his time!

SECTION TEN:

time to bin a few things

22. this is not going to be easy

So... what now?

Not easy to continue after the razzmatazz of teddy bears, Jedi knights and porn. But we have to try.

Well, for starters, we need to clear away the dead wood. The 21st century has no time for stuff which passed muster in the 70s, 80s, 90s or even the noughties. It is a whole new world order out there, a world where the brand, the bear and image mean everything.

We have already listed the various areas that are considered the foundation of postmodernist marketing and have had a good attempt at showing a few practical anti-marketing methods of selling.

So, at this juncture, let us throw a few things away. We need to clear the decks a little.

So... here are a few binnable things:

- **That the product is the most important thing**
- **The Ps, Es, Ns and Qs do not mean a thing anymore**
- **That the customer is always right**
- **That choice is great**
- **That to have the best does not mean you will be the most successful**
- **That cheap prices are the answer**

- **That people are sensible**
- **All books on marketing (except one)**

Throw the lot away. Bin them all.

Because none of them have any relevance to what is going on out there. Let me explain…

The product really does not matter. The only thing that does is the brand or perception of what the brand is. The Ps have ceased to be important, as the Internet blurs all boundaries, quite spectacularly.

The customer is never right, because he/she can only really understand what he/she knows now, not what the future may bring. He/she is generally not a very intelligent creature either, always deferring to the lowest common denominator when it comes to buying habits.

Multiple choice in the market place is not necessarily a good thing either and having the best stuff out there will never guarantee success and riches. If you have the loudest voice and the most money, you will generally get your products sold, whatever the quality. The best will always be beaten by the average (with a wad of cash behind it).

And… don't think that big discounts and wall-to-wall sales will solve your problems. They won't. They will only delay the inevitable, because cheap things never make money. They only serve to clear unsellable shelves of outdated products.

Finally, there are the many books on marketing out there. Most are dull, a lot are misleading, some are vaguely interesting, a few are humorous and only one or two hit the mark.

Stark Reality

So, where are we in the grand scheme of things and what do customers now expect from businesses?

First, 24-hour service is standard in today's marketplace and nothing special. People expect to be able to buy stuff round the clock and will walk if kept waiting for more than a nanosecond. The online revolution has made customers impatient, selfish, spoilt and totally disloyal. They will disappear for the smallest and most insignificant reason.

As for after-sales service, people expect a 100% refund if not entirely satisfied. In fact, there is a growing segment of the customer-base that actively 'buys' stuff online, with no intention of keeping it. We are rapidly becoming a nation of online 'browser-buyers', who return 90% of goods. 'Returns' have made parcel delivery services very profitable and has breathed new life into the post office.

Customers have seen and heard it all before.

Customers have become inured to the traditional sales machine and 'not-to-be-missed' offer. Why? Simply because the online revolution throws constant sales opportunities at them pretty much every minute of the day and night. It is a relentless barrage from the moment a potential customer opens his or her eyes in the morning, till the time the light goes out at night.

This might all be seen as wonderfully convenient, but then then the reality of the intrusive, digital marketing juggernaut dawns on most people. And the saner ones begin to hate it.

Sellers can forget trends and predictive forecasting too

Because it is a jungle out there. Too much to analyse and too much information. Statistics can prove or disprove virtually anything we like.

Worse still, it can upset the customer, as well. For example, I bought a pair of gloves last year from Amazon. Fine – they are really good and did the trick perfectly on cold days. But now, almost every day, Amazon feeds me information on gloves of all descriptions, whenever I log on. I do not want any more gloves. One pair is enough – I do not want to buy a pair every other minute. This upsets me and actually puts me off buying stuff from Amazon, especially presents for other people.

Another apocalyptic example. I bought an unbelievably horrible ceramic rabbit for a friend three years ago – and even today I am still reminded of this unwise decision. Amazon seems to think I am now in the market for anything vaguely ceramic… and tasteless. The fact that I sent it straight to this friend and listed it as a gift, means nothing to the good people in Amazon marketing. They now believe that leering ceramic hedgehogs, horses, meerkats, frogs, pandas, foxes, squirrels, dogs, cats and on one appalling occasion, a blue dachshund, are part and parcel of my usual shopping habits with them.

We all like to be masters of our own destiny. To be able to turn our laptop on, click our mobile into action and to play the game of marketing by our own rules. To be able to buy stuff regularly or on a whim, but not to live to regret it for months or even years, afterwards.

One final and more serious example of all this. I made the error of sending an online birthday card to my mother in 2008. I was living in China at the time, so could not rely on the postal system for a proper card. So, I sent the online card via a popular e-card website... and all was fine. My mother received it and was duly appreciative.

Then the problems began. The online ecard company I had used, logged all my mother's details (as well as my own) onto their database and has, since that first apocalyptic e-card, sent me reminders to send a message/card to my mother for every possible festival or event, ever since. Now normally, I would not mind, but my mother died in 2013, so to receive reminders of Mother's Day every year after that, is both insensitive and upsetting. I have tried unsubscribing but, like a weed in a garden, after a month or two of nothing, the reminders start up again.

Segmentation on a very individual level can be both intrusive and counter-productive. Segmentation on a more 'generalised' level, where people's buying habits are predicted as a mass might work better, but can still be misleading.

One simple rule of thumb

This new age also has a new mantra. It is no longer product, price, clever segmentation, the loudness of your shout in the marketplace, fluff, or anything else that matters most. Whatever you are selling in today's cyber world, you just need to have one vital ingredient:

SPEED

If you manage that with your sales processes, then you are halfway to being successful. If you do not, you will fail. Better to be fast than good. People want instant everything, even if they have to sacrifice quality.

The McDonald's promise in Japanese restaurants

And, of course, this has made us a very impatient and ungrateful society. In the past, you spent your life waiting for things. In shops, banks, post offices, at ticket offices in theatres, stations, sports venues etc.

We learned that patience is a virtue. Not so, nowadays. Better to be quick and second-rate, than slow and fantastic.

Small digression. I recently lived for 10 years in a city called Suzhou in China – a city which does not even merit a place on most world maps and yet had a population of 7 million when I was there. And I realised during my time there that the Chinese have infinite patience.

It was like stepping back in time when I witnessed people queuing for pretty-much everything. At banks, coffee shops, restaurants, airports and hairdressers. I have even seen people queueing for over a day for a train ticket.

When I was there, the Internet was in its infancy, servers were chronically slow, modems were always going 'offline' and many foreign sites had government restrictions slapped on them. It was still a society which, to all intents and purposes, existed in the 70s and was struggling painfully to get to grips with the digital age in practical (and political) terms.

The irony was that Chinese companies produced most of the world's latest, cutting-edge technology - from computers to mobile phones. And yet, the man or woman on the Beijing omnibus was unable to utilise most of these developments the way we do in the west.

Of course, there are political considerations to take into account here, as well as the small technical issue of getting nearly 2 billion people online and keeping them there without 'crashes' all the time. Are the Chinese unhappy about this? Not at all. They are a patient lot by nature and, on the rare occasion that they actually do get something quickly, it is a bonus - not a requirement.

In fact, if you told the average Chinese person that it was possible to order anything (from a book to a refrigerator) on a Monday and then receive it later that day or the next day, most of them would laugh at you. This was still a pre-digital culture, in most practical ways.

But western culture is not. Speed is the name of the game and we expect stuff to be on our doorstep almost before we think of it. It is getting as bad as that. And the largest and most successful companies are the ones that are the quickest. Some pizza delivery companies now offer you a free pizza if they take more than 30 minutes to get a pepperoni thin-crust to your door in time. Others give you a massive discount or even an extra (free) dish for any delay, no matter how slight. And Amazon, of course, can get books to you a few hours after you have bought them. You can even sidestep the whole delivery process completely and download stuff instantly, if you have zero patience. This goes for movies, music and games as well.

I started my own company in 2014 (*supercourses.co.uk*) which promised students the best possible price for English courses at English language schools in the UK. It sounded like a pretty-good idea (along the lines of 'Booking.com' and 'Trivago') and I was already a millionaire in my own mind and ordering bright red Ferraris, before we went 'live'. We even went so far as to offer a totally free service to all students, we were that confident.

First indications were positive – we had dozens of students registering on our site, requesting everything from English courses in Liverpool for 4 weeks, to business English in Brighton for 36 weeks.

Now, the core of the site, the beating heart, is that a student's request is channelled to all the schools on our database in the student's chosen location. Schools then come back to the site with their 'best offer'. Fantastic idea. Couldn't fail.

And we did receive bookings too. But… not that many at the beginning. Why? Because students expected an instant price when they hit the 'confirm-a-course' button. The idea of having to wait even a few seconds, was an anathema and they clicked away in droves. Even when 'offers' from schools eventually came in (always within a day), students had already drifted to other sites or lost interest. And ironically, these offers were great. Some schools offered over 20% discount.

We found that a notable number of students had even gone ahead and booked courses at schools which gave them the standard price without a discount. The fact that these same schools were on our site and, if the student had waited a few short minutes, he/she would have been offered 20% discount, did not seem to matter. Speed trumped saving money most of the time.

So, it would appear that the more digital the society, the more that quality and price are compromised, because speed is now the major player in the game. If you live in an essentially pre-digital society, like China, you still can argue over quality, price and service, because speed is not an issue at all… yet.

So, what can we do?

Quite simply, we have to understand postmodernist marketing (or anti-marketing or anti-selling) a little better, if we are to grapple with the 21st century customer. He or she is a simple creature, which does irrational things for what would appear daft reasons. And so, the marketing and sales person has to think chaotically too. To think differently. Laterally. And to embrace warmly a Pandora's Box of contradictory ideas.

SECTION ELEVEN:

the top ten anti-commandments

23. The top ten

- Think of something genuinely and radically different as your USP (look at your competitors' lists and bin any of yours that remotely resemble theirs)

- Give simple, clear information (make it very short and childishly simple)

- Make it current (no one remembers what happened yesterday – people today have the memory of a goldfish)

- Make it relevant to today's customer (which means making it very low culture)

- Break down boundaries (there are no rules anymore – do anything to make a splash and to hell with the consequences. Those are tomorrow's problems)

- Be scrupulously open and honest (no half-truths either) even if this may initially harm sales

- Do the dangerous and risky thing (never take the tried-and-tested, easy route)

- Don't be afraid to walk away from any deal or customer (it shows strength of character and supreme confidence)

- Don't do the same thing year after year and expect business to improve (Einstein once said

that the definition of madness was doing the
same thing over and over and expecting
different results)

- Embrace your weak points (broadcast your
failings and weaknesses loudly and be proud of
them)

- React quickly to all situations (instant is the
way of things, nowadays – better a quick, bad
decision than a delayed, right one)

- Attract the customer rather than promote to him
(make the customer come to you and feel
wanted, loved, cosseted and part of your team)

- Make it fun for everyone (staff, colleagues and
customers, of course)

- Tell a story if all else fails (people remember
stories, not bullet points – like these. I
guarantee that you will have forgotten all the
points on these two pages by page 287). Don't
worry – there will be a reminder waiting for you
there). Sometimes you have to be cruel to be
kind...

- Don't get bogged down analysing in the old
ways (SWOT, PESTLE etc.) because they are a
waste of time and effort and mean very little in
today's market-place

- Whatever you do, be FAST... very FAST,
ridiculously FAST

- **And always have a bag of bears by your side –
  they will inevitably play their part at some stage**

OK – so, it's not 10, but saying the '17 Commandments' would not carry as much gravitas. Most of these points are pretty self-explanatory and are not that revolutionary. We have also touched on most of them already.

Some marketeers (traditional ones too) would just say that many of them are just good, solid, sane marketing (OK, not all of them) in an age which demands so much. Nothing that postmodern at all. I would accept that, but would contend that few businesses actually put more than 5 or 6 of these into practice. Old habits die hard (I have said that before, too).

As for the customer him or herself, he or she is a mixed back of contradictions, who is easily offended, always suspicious and extremely reticent at taking his or her wallet or purse out, no matter what the reason is. That is just the way of the world in today's society.

Another angle on customer suspicion

A television station conducted an interesting experiment recently. A reporter wandered the streets of a well-known UK city and offered every passer-by a free ten-pound note. No strings, no catches. It was just a free ten-pound note. A present. A gift. For nothing. Remarkably, almost everyone refused it. Why? Because no one ever believes that you get something for nothing nowadays. There had to be a catch. There had to be a reason. People waved him away and walked on. A policeman even arrived on the scene and asked what was going on, believing that the reporter was out to scam or con the public in some novel and rather odd way. We are living in a society where simple acts of kindness simply do not happen very often… and when they do, we just do not believe them.

Wrapping this bit up

It could be argued that my off-piste, postmodernist, anti-marketing commandments above have become essential in today's marketing not because marketing and sales people have suddenly become self-righteous, kind, lovable and considerate. It is simply because you cannot get away with being vaguely naughty or selective with the truth anymore. The 'commandments' cover so many aspects of 'unusual' marketing, not just being totally honest, superhero fast and unexpectedly nice. Being different, clear, simple, current, relevant, dangerous, brave, fun and not afraid to step away from the deal, are steps too far for many sales people who prefer a solid, tried-and-tested, traditional marketing approach.

The sad reality is that businesses will have to adopt some (if not all) of these commandments, if they are to survive in the 21st century as the Internet increases its grip on business's throats.

SECTION TWELVE:

how to use anti-marketing

24. and now for something completely different

The essence of postmodernist, anti-marketing is to do the thing that no one would expect, to play with your customers' worst fears and then make a joke about it all. It is to emphasise weak points and downplay strengths; to view threats in a positive way and then to see choice as possibly a bad thing.

Marketing and sales in the 21st century is both incredibly simple and confusingly complicated at the same time. If you try to over-think it then you will fail, but if you approach it the way a customer (or child) would, then it is extremely easy.

Basically, anti-marketing is a combination of contradictions, which should not work in any sane way at all. However, it (sometimes) does. Why? Because we are dealing with human beings, who have illogical, unreasonable and very different personalities.

The fundamental mistake of past, traditional marketing theories was that they considered human beings as essentially logical, rational and sane. Customers, when given a variety of choices, would invariably weigh up all the options and then make the best possible selection. That is what marketing people liked to think and this is what statistics and analyses relied upon.

As we all know, customers today rarely make decisions based on all the facts available and are never logical. Today's customer is ruled by subjective emotions of the moment. And, no matter how hard you try to map the 'customer journey', or draw up endless 'spending-habit' spreadsheets, the customer usually ends up jumping in an entirely different direction than predicted. A marketing person of today has to think on his or her feet more than ever before. Openness, simplicity and clarity, moulded with honesty, truth and speed are the cornerstones of modern sales and marketing.

No marketing person really has any idea what is happening anymore, if he or she is being totally honest. We may have bright ideas, great plans and grand strategies but, at the end of a long day, it is all still very hit-or-miss as to whether our businesses will succeed or fail. And the Internet has made the whole arena of marketing a very unstable, yet amazingly exciting place to be.

And that's about it.

So, be dangerous, honest, quick, remarkable and have a bit of fun!

It's your turn now

We now reach that moment when we look at some practical examples of postmodern, anti-marketing, which have appeared on our streets, televisions and on billboards over the past few years.

Some are very relevant to what has been discussed, some are marginally relevant, some are contentious, some teeter on the edge of being repetitive, some are funny, some are silly, some are astonishing, some are a little boring and some are just plain, good marketing, if seen from a very oblique angle.

All are in the arena of anti-marketing and are designed to make you think and laugh (or both), at the same time.

And… because this is postmodernist anti-marketing, where reverse psychology rubs shoulders with principled/relationship/engagement/ethical and sacred selling and marketing; and where such entities as anti-foundationalism/ retrospection/ paradoxical juxtaposition/ parody and pastiche are the general loose headings under which the whole thing is categorised, I would like you (dear reader) to get involved and take part in the process. To be part of the handbook and not just the end product – a very postmodernist gesture (if you had not worked that out already).

'Decentering' and 'reversal' on a massive, fragmented level where readers (high and low cultures merging seamlessly as one) have assumed a major role in a self-referential expansion of this handbook!

So, read carefully, please

What follows are TWENTY pretty good examples of what it is all about. I have placed at the top of each, my own suggestions as to why I think these are great examples of anti-marketing. By their nature, these are very loose categorizations.

Now comes your bit.

I have added 3 extra ones at the end (without my comments at all), which I am inviting you (the reader) to categorise and explain.

Please contact me with your 'ideas' (adrianliley@hotmail.com) and I will give the best, most succinct and hopefully witty ones, 'credit' in subsequent editions, should this handbook ever make it that far!

I would also like to invite you to send me your own photos which demonstrate different aspects of postmodern, anti-marketing. And, if you think you know of other areas which should be included in a handbook on this amazing subject, then please let me know.

You then really will be part of the whole process of building this handbook, which is as it should be - a harmony of disharmony!

26. hitting the street

ONE: Sell your worst points

Parody/ Anti-Foundationalism / Reverse Psychology / Defensive Pessimism

Let's start with a really good one. This poster at Prague airport concerns the second ugliest building in the world. Yes, the second. Not the ugliest, but the second ugliest. It's funny, clever and brutally, cruelly, truthful. The building is horrible. They know it. You know it. We all know it. It even has small, metallic, black babies crawling up and down its exterior. Clearly, previous positive marketing of the place has failed. It also even leaves you wondering where the ugliest building is…

The **ZIZKOV TELEVISION TOWER in PRAGUE**

TWO: Be dangerous

De-Differentiation / Parody / Storytelling / Paradoxical
Juxtaposition/ Shock

The English language industry also dabbles in 'dangerous' marketing at times. To be able to shock and then create discussion can only increase awareness of a brand in a crowded market. The London School of English certainly managed this with a brochure which broke away from standard norms quite spectacularly. Instead of pictures of happy, smiling students or sunny pictures of the school itself, the marketing team put up a picture of a chimpanzee. The inside pages continued with the same theme of 'Let's talk about monkeys'. In a way, it was juxtaposition meets de-differentiation with lots of parody thrown in for good measure. Many hated the idea, some considered it bad taste, a few thought it ridiculous and one or two even said it was racist. No one ignored it, because it trod the edges of acceptability by being clever, thought-provoking, humorous and… different.

Let's talk about monkeys.

THREE: No name is the name
Minimalist / Principled / Decentering

The craze in Japan and then America a few years ago was to wear clothes without visible logos. It was a startling move for retailers in a world where outward branding was the norm. But the plain designs were an instant hit with a section of society tired of being a walking billboard for big corporations or designers. A few years ago, an excellent restaurant in Great Queen Street, London, was only known for its food and… not having a name. It relied on word-of-mouth recommendation and filled every night. This was one of the purest forms of anti-marketing in that it had no name, no real logo apart from a small knife and fork image and a crown, to reflect that it was in Great Queen Street. And a street address, nothing else.

FOUR: Being the bad boy works, too
Reverse Psychology / Relationship / Shock / 'Dark' / Parody

Everyone tries to cast a positive slant on their products and wares. It is only natural. You want people to like what you are doing and to approve of your stuff. Wrong. Sometimes, adopting the opposite standpoint will serve you better and make people stop in their tracks. Take the clothing retailer, 'French Connection', and their bold decision to use 'FCUK' as their logo a few years ago. Imagine the shock and horror in the French Connection boardroom on the day that their brave marketing manager unveiled that campaign. And take the owners of the record shop in downtown Reykjavik, Iceland (the picture below). Perhaps they are on safer ground here, since the music industry is renowned for its rebelliousness. Selling your 'bad taste' items can only increase your standing, because it means cutting-edge, anti-establishment, music.

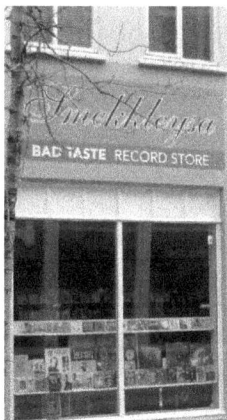

(picture taken by Steve Liley, my brother, while on holiday and researching his latest novel – 'Olaf's Saga' – available at all good booksellers!)

FIVE: Star your Weaknesses
Defensive Pessimism / Principled / Trust-Based / De-Differentiation

There will always come a time when a marketing team looks at their product and wonders how to hide a defect, or something that might harm sales. It is always very tempting to go down the 'concealment' path. A few years ago, I was in a marketing team that had a summer junior centre at Brighton University. It looked great from almost every angle, except for the one irritating point that the campus was split up into three very different areas, a few miles apart. So, the big question was: do we hide this when selling to agents and students? Our marketing manager decided, on a whim, not just to tell potential students about the need for a bus to take them all over Brighton for their lessons, food and sports, but to 'star' this weakness as a major feature - in effect, turning the whole problem on its head and making it a strength. The marketing campaign started with the headline: 'Ride the Big Lemon!' The result was happy children and agents, who knew what to expect when they arrived and were actually looking forward to the inconvenience!

(All credit to Santi Brea Moriscot - the Marketing Manager concerned, at British Study Centres)

SIX: Threaten your possible customers with an early death

Shock / De-Differentiation / Ethical / Parody / Paradoxical Juxtaposition

It doesn't harm to go the whole hog and scare your customers to death, especially if it's for their own good! Campaigns about stopping smoking, road safety and excessive drinking are the best examples here. The poster below was part of an Italian 'get-fit' campaign and is not only a humorous image Michelangelo's iconic statue of David, but also could be seen as a great example of de-differentiation in its mixing of high and low culture. It gets the obesity message across in a somewhat brutal way too.

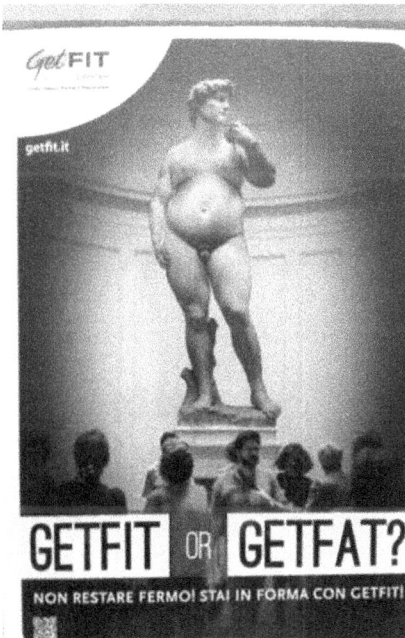

SEVEN: Something totally unique
Relationship / Engagement / Trust-Based / Reversal

This is easier said than done. Many businesses list their USPs which, to be honest, are not that unique at all. But…if you can find something that truly puts you ahead of the crowd and makes you remarkable, then you should immediately star it. The Excel School of English in north London had this great idea a few years ago. Every student who studied there, was given a free mug on arrival which they could sign and personalise. Not only did students feel part of the school community seeing it hanging there in the school café, but visitors to the school were immediately impressed by the number of students at the school. Simple, easy and effective marketing. And completely unique… at that time.

EIGHT: Embrace your unpopularity
Reverse Psychology / Parody / 'Accidental' / 'Shock'

Sometimes, being out-of-fashion is not necessarily a bad thing. Again, marketing shows its obtuse side. A company will never deliberately set out to sell unfashionable products and yet, as marketing people know, anything is possible, if given the right 'spin'. The shop in the picture below (in Suzhou, deepest China), clearly had a very brave owner. To call his outlet '*Non-Trend*' was a bold move, however you look at it. But, thinking deviously, this is China – a place where people try to conform as much as possible. Perhaps being 'non-trend' was a trend in itself – a trend for conformity. Either that or the owner simply had mis-used his English and the fascia was meant to read 'On-Trend'. Usage of English in China is 'elastic' at the best of times. I remember seeing one of those 'Baby on Board' stickers in a car, rear-view mirror. The one difference was that it read: 'Baby on Road'.

NINE: Attack your own stuff
Shock / Reverse Psychology / Parody

When you are advertising your products, you have to be innovative and deviously clever. If people simply dismiss your offering without a second thought, then you have lost. Ironically, if you resort to shouting loudly how fantastic you are, people will still just walk past. No one believes anyone who promotes their stuff as being the best, anymore. After all, everyone says this and it is never true. The public have been moulded by marketing people into a very cynical bunch. So, attack your own product, mercilessly. And then leave it at that. No small print either, which somehow explains the joke. If you are big enough and have a massive slice of the market, then this is easier to do. People already know your product, so the risk is minimal. If you are new to the market and vulnerably small, then such a tactic can be dangerous, but is infinitely better in the long run, because it makes a splash and people always remember the surprising thing.

Sky Arts relaunched their channel with these large posters, this one emblazoned all over Bromley South railway station.

TEN: The personal touch
Principled / Engagement / Relationship / Trust-Based

Make it personal and avoid the template as much as possible. This may be impossible if you own a massive corporation, but there are ways of making each customer feel important. Special. The makers of Pokemon Go (Niantic) have an excellent system of reply 'bots' which handle most issues in a very 'human' way. Businesses that only use 'bounce-back' emails, or 'no-reply' automated responses, inevitably frustrate and annoy the 21st century customer. I recently bought a board game for my nephew and niece from a company via Amazon. I received a well-wrapped parcel just two days later with a personal letter inside from the company owner and her own email address. Now this tells me that either this company has very few customers and can afford the time to do this, or they have an amazing director who sees every customer as gold dust. Whatever – this was incredible after-sales service!

Hi Adnan,

I would like to thank you for your order and hope that you have been satisfied with the service provided.

As a small seller the provision of feedback on Amazon is a means by which I am able to monitor delivery times and so help in my continued commitment in trying to provide excellent customer service.

If there have been any issues concerning your order please feel free to email me in the first instance

Yours sincerely

ELEVEN: Sell something else

Storytelling/ Pastiche / Plurivalence

You would be kidding yourself if you did not believe that English language courses are a very dry subject to market and sell. There really isn't a lot of difference between one school and another when it comes to actual lesson content. So, how do you make your product stand out and be different? The London School of English (following up on their monkey brochure) had a fantastic chef in their school restaurant a few years ago and so set about creating a novel brochure which 'starred' all the staff's favourite dishes from the weekly menu. There wasn't a mention of English courses in the brochure – just page after page of mouth-watering delicacies and staff comments. This was something genuinely different. The moral is simple. Find something totally unique, then shout about it, even if it has absolutely nothing to do with your core business.

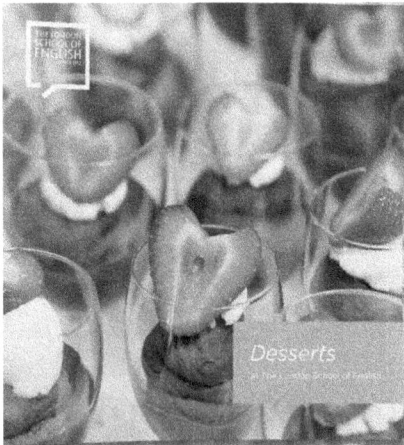

TWELVE: Tell your customers about a problem, even before it exists
Defensive Pessimism/ Self-Referentiality

Customers are always complaining about the trains. It is probably the second most moaned about thing (after the weather). And one issue, more than most, always causes irritation, humour and frustration. The annual horror of 'leaves on the line' delays train services (in the UK) and is usually met with half-hearted official excuses along the lines of heavy winds, too many trees falling at once, sticky leaves and even the 'wrong kind' of trees. But recently, an official campaign (the poster below) was launched by the train authorities in the south-east of England. It is clever, pre-emptive marketing, because it addresses a problem, before it exists. People are far more understanding if told all about a possible issue before it happens. It is somehow reassuring, although I am intrigued by the fact that they have some official counting the leaves that drop on our lines.

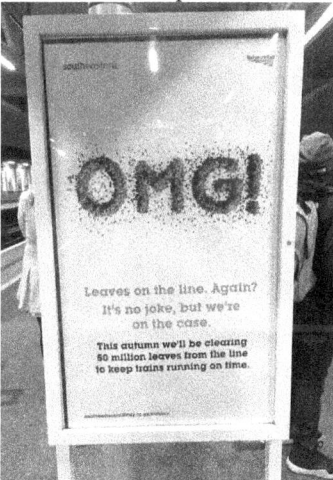

THIRTEEN: Be really dangerous
Reverse Psychology / 'Light Dark' / Parody / Anti-Foundationalism

Taking a leap into the unknown can be a daunting and expensive way to go, especially in marketing. It can reap amazing dividends, or it can fall flat on its face. There is no middle course. But, to do the spectacularly dangerous is to be admired, whatever happens. I passed a restaurant in Manchester recently, which grabbed my attention. It stopped me dead in my tracks. I had to take a photo of it and then go inside and have a look. I ended up having something to eat in there as well… and it was very nice, too. But can you imagine the initial meeting when the person with the bright idea to call a café *'fatso's'*, pitched it to potential investors? There are so many reasons that such a name would cause offence or upset people. There are precedents, of course, like the successful clothing retailer, 'Fat Face' or the café that sells 'Fatburgers'. Whatever the reasoning behind these controversial names, you have to admire the gall of going down such a route.

FOURTEEN: Sell it how it is, warts and all

Principled / 'Shock' / Engagement / Parody / Anti-Foundationalism

A few years ago, the language school, International House Newcastle, decided to change their brochure. Why? Because the old one was simply not cutting the mustard. Student numbers were low and people shied away from the cold, wild and woolly north of England. Students preferred the warmer south. So, how could Newcastle and the surrounding area compete with London, Brighton, Cambridge and Oxford? The two owners came up with a novel idea. Simply tell it how it is. So, they created the 'One Step Further' campaign, immediately ditching most of the text inside and replacing it with huge photo spreads. What followed was possibly the first use of 'visual storytelling' in the industry - combined with total honesty. The pictures concentrated on the surrounding countryside on dark, rainy days, forbidding mediaeval castles and gun-metal skies. The effect was startling. And successful. Suddenly, a new type of student emerged - a student who wanted adventure, history and the 'real' England; a student who did not want sandy beaches or tourist-filled cities. A student who wanted the truth!

FIFTEEN: Angels with Incontinence
Plurivalence / Paradoxical Juxtaposition / Hyper-Reality / Parody /
'Mildly Dark' / Principled / Storytelling / Shock / De-
Differentiation

Sometimes, when you have a product which is of a purely practical nature and has no real glamour or appeal at all, you have to create your own 'buzz'. Underwear which deals with incontinence must fall into this category. You can either go down the strictly medical route, or you can take the anti-marketing path. The poster below is a great example of combining several anti-marketing features. First, Tena (the company) uses a completely different type of fashion model (i.e. not a ridiculously thin woman). Second, to give the model white angel wings (contrasting to the black lingerie), a coquettish expression, high heels, and then to put it all under the banner headline: '*Secret's Out*', hints at naughtiness from even the purest of beings. The implication here is that angels have bladder problems, too. Suddenly, you have a completely different type of advertisement, where the actual product is almost forgotten in the swirling contradictions of the image. High culture (angelic being) meets very low culture (bladder trouble and 'naughtiness'), while being barrier-breaking, controversial and startlingly different.

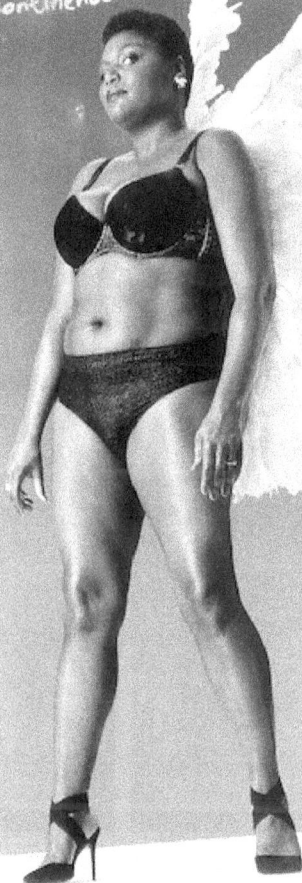

SECRET'S OUT
1 in 3 women have
incontinence

NEW SILHOUETTE
NOIR UNDERWEAR

TENA

277

SIXTEEN: Hard-hitting, public-interest advertising
Shock / Ethical / Principled / Dark

Back in the 70s, successive governments suddenly slowly began to accept that allowing advertising of harmful pursuits like smoking and drinking might have an adverse effect on voting patterns in the long run. So, the mood changed with drastic attempts to warn people of the health hazards of smoking and drinking. Since that time, other anti-social activities (see below for fly-tipping and needless speeding) have been attacked – by using clever 'Big Brother' tactics. This is 'schockvertising' in its rawest form - the 'eye' of society watching you in one poster, while the foot of retribution squashing you in the other.

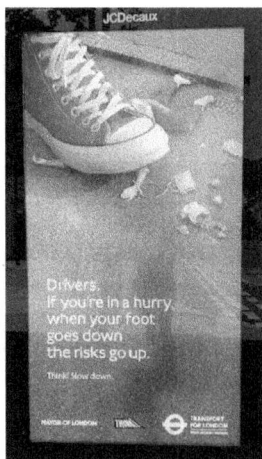

SEVENTEEN: 'Wackaging' still works
Storytelling / Ethical / Pastiche / Parody

Wackaging (wacky packaging) came about in the early noughties with companies using their wrappers or packaging to 'talk' to the customer - to make friends and be as humorous as possible. It was mostly embraced by companies on an ethical or green mission. It seemed that saving the planet went hand-in-hand with healthy food and drink. 'Innocent' was probably the first to use this marketing technique with their tongue-in-cheek 'stories' on their drinks' labels, but others like 'Rude Health' (below) followed suit very quickly. Not content with describing the contents of their milk alternative, they tried to explain what rude health was in a more 'alternative' way. It is parody, pastiche and humour all on a simple label.

RUDE HEALTH

To be in rude health is an old english expression meaning up for life and bursting with energy.

You're in rude health when...
you've pole danced on a lamp-post. You ferment your own kimchi. You pack a skipping rope on a business trip.

EIGHTEEN: Sell to the 14th century client!

Storytelling / Pastiche / Parody / Trust-Based / Retrospection

Sometimes, the anti-marketeer has to go right to the very edge of understanding and meaning. But, when you have a business based in the mediaeval town of Tewkesbury, then you can be forgiven. The solicitors below decided to 'jazz' up their brochure advertisement, by theming their wares for the 14th century client. It is not only clever, but also humorous, extremely retro and pokes fun at itself. Even the language used is designed to be 'olde' fashioned. What's more, it makes the reader want to read more. Had the solicitors' simply gone down the usual route, then readers flicking through the brochure would have barely given it a second glance. Even encouraging people to look at their website is brilliantly worded: *'Looketh upon our wares'*.

NINETEEN: Mix it all up!

When you have a large business, an equally large
advertising budget and lots of freedom to do the
unusual, then you have the right ingredients to mix
everything up. The recent television AA (Automobile
Association) commercial combined humour, parody
and a clever mixture of reality with hyper-reality to
create a 30 second piece of genius. The science fiction
parody, 'Red Dwarf', is used as the vehicle here to sell
AA services. Basically, the space ship has broken
down and Lister calls the AA breakdown service for
help. And, lo and behold, a black woman (not the
traditional image of a white man with a spanner),
appears thousands of years in the future in an AA
space ship and solves the problem. And just to add
the postmodern cherry to the cake, there is not even a
mention of cars, or any car images in the entire
commercial. We have hyper-reality selling a service
that does not exist (space ship repairs) by a black
woman who manages to transverse time and space.
Brilliant!

TWENTY: Urban street talk helps the 'teen' market

Relationship / Engagement / De-Differentiation / Paradoxical Juxtaposition

It has always been the case that in the never-ending war between Coca-Cola and Pepsi, that Coke goes for the slightly older, patriotic market (particularly in the USA) while Pepsi sees its target market as younger people. Coca Cola tried to combat this mind-set recently with a campaign aimed specifically at teens using urban street-talk which pretty-much only they would understand.

The genius of the campaign was then to make a series of TV commercials using 'senior' citizens flicking through a 'Tinder' like app on their mobile phones. This is a great example of mixing stereotypes and aims at telling customers that we are all 'teens' at heart, no matter what the age.

TWENTY-ONE:

Now it's your turn:

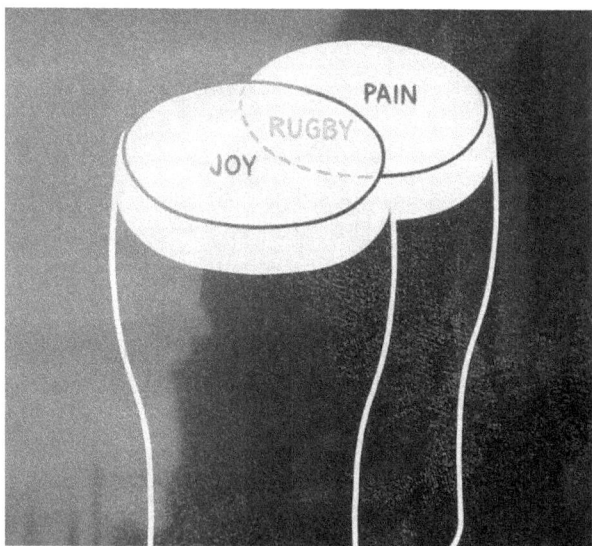

TWENTY-TWO

TWEBNTY-THREE:

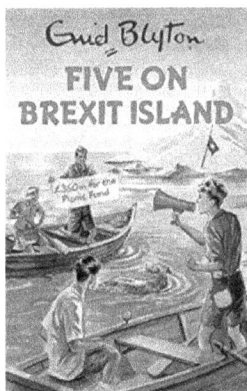

Gnid Blyton
FIVE ON
BREXIT ISLAND

Gnid Blyton
FIVE GIVE UP
THE BOOZE

SECTION THIRTEEN:

Final thoughts

27. the end

... well, nearly

(and this is the promised moment.
How many of you remember any of the bullet-pointed
Top Ten Anti-Commandments on Page 254? On the
other hand, do you remember what Teddy Bear Wars
was all about?)

"Oh Lord! Do we have the strength to pull off this mighty task in one night... or are we just jerking off?"

(The Reverend Johnson, from 'Blazing Saddles'. 1974.
Another quote – I lied)

So, there it is. Postmodernism and anti-marketing in a nut-shell - a mish-mash of semi-serious explanations, a few contentious assertions, some solid examples from the street, heaps of repetition and the odd story thrown in. So, how can we finish this minor epic on the paper castles of postmodernism and its relevance to marketing and sales?

A quick recap...

Postmodernism is a very slippery subject. Well, it defies definition – in fact, it has been argued that trying to define it, blunts its impact. After all, postmodernism, by its very nature, is a rejection of order and conceptualization. It is a grey, opaque mist at the best of times – a murky pool of contradictions, at worst.

Another problem with categorising postmodernism is that definitions vary from author to author. The more creative and daring among us simply accept that it is a very human concept and see it as a necessary counter to the modernist age.

So, we can now drift, happily rudderless, into regions populated by what some people call 'relativists'.

Sorry, this is a new term not mentioned previously, just rather rudely slipped in at the end. Bear with me again, please. It is a very brief interruption.

Relativists believe that no knowledge or beliefs (whatever the society or culture) are superior or inferior to one another. All are valid and should be respected as such. And, as a beautiful postmodern consequence, nothing can be compared, categorised or segmented, because everything is equal, right and wrong, good and bad... Relativists are postmodernism's best friend.

Postmodernism is different things to different people

And it is not just a matter of thrashing out some sort of compromise definition either, because postmodernism means different things to different people in different genres.

In architecture, form, logic, angles and exactitude seem to symbolise modernism (e.g. the old Trade

Towers in New York and perhaps Centre Point in London), while postmodernism is exciting, strange and perhaps more appropriate to the surrounding landscape. Just look at the Guggenheim in Bilbao, or even the Sydney Opera House. Both broke new ground when it came to design and made a provocative statement about what could be done with engineering and art in the 20th century.

I myself have always viewed postmodernist architecture as the sort of stuff which bends angles, creates optical illusions and fashions buildings to look as if they are going to collapse spectacularly at any given moment.

On the silver screen, there are so many examples of postmodernist films and television programmes and how they have shaped what we see today. Let us look at one last example (not mentioned before and a great one, which I have been dying to talk about). Mel Brooks produced *'Blazing Saddles'* in 1974, hot on the heels of his provocative and controversial movie, *'The Producers'*. Both stretched the boundaries of convention to snapping point – some would say that Brooks actually snapped it several times, glued it back together and then snapped it again.

"How many times have I told you to wash up after a weekly cross burning?"

'Blazing Saddles' broke every rule, faced racism brutally and head-on, as well as ridiculing the musical, the western and the big budget 'Busby-Berkeley' spectacular. It set itself up as a parody of the western at the start (most notably with the 'beans'

scene); then picked up pace by tearing apart 70s attitudes to native Americans and race. The selection of a black sheriff turned convention on its head, empowering a repressed race and then positioning it in direct confrontation with middle-class, Bible-belt America. The startling expletive from a little old white lady ('Up yours, n*****!') is not only appalling in itself, but sums up what Brooks calls the 'moronic' people of 'the land'.

The whole movie has chaos and absurdity stamped all over it from the ridiculous overnight building of a 'fake' town to fool the bandits to the mass fight at the end involving every genre you could imagine - even WW2 German Stormtroopers and Ku Klux Klan members. The ending even surpassed '*Springtime for Hitler*' in '*The Producers*'.

And then, (I haven't finished yet) with the fight at the end of the film getting completely out of hand, all the characters break out of the film itself and start invading other film sets including the Busby-Berkeley one, where the great line: "*P*** off, we're working for Mel Brooks!*" is uttered. We finally have the main characters running down a Hollywood street to a nearby theatre to catch the ending of *Blazing Saddles*! It is not only brutal anti-foundationalism with shades of de-differentiation, parody and pastiche thrown in for good measure, but then, as a cherry on this daft cake, it all ends by being sublimely self-referential.

But all this is wandering far from the point.

Sorry, I am really dragging this ending out. Think 'Lord of the Rings'... third film

Postmodernism values spontaneity, individuality, creativity and the human illogicality rubbing shoulders with irony, irreverence and cynicism in both positive and negative ways. It is an elevation of the 'human spirit' to the very centre of the whole process, while cavalierly playing with meta-narratives, convention and genre – or something like that.

As you can see, it is easy to drift into simplistic platitudes, just as it is easy to over-complicate the beast. And that is the conundrum. It has been said that postmodernism is a 'portmanteau' term which carries a variety of sins in its baggage, encapsulating anything that cannot be categorised or neatly filed away. A hotchpotch. Perhaps that is the best way of describing it.

It is also an infuriating subject which appears happiest when being contradictory, provocative, silly and preoccupied with ambiguity.

Postmodernist marketing

Put into the context of marketing, postmodernism is all of the above – it can be viewed as exciting, ground-breaking, remarkable, as well as being chaotic and unstable - existing in a world where we believe that anything goes. And it could also be a combination of sarcasm, cynicism, nihilism, truth, honesty and total self-belief. Or it could just be a nice, humorous, harmless distraction, which adds a bit of colour to the ultimately dull and dry world of marketing and sales.

BUT... throw the Internet into the mix and suddenly postmodernist marketing assumes a greater prominence in the game. This, as has been said previously, has become the game-changer. The Internet has made all things possible on an instantaneous global scale.

As for anti-marketing...

...this is another puzzle, wrapped in a riddle. I said many pages ago that I consider both anti-marketing and postmodernist marketing as synonymous in today's market place. Obviously, it can be claimed that there are differences, which I have already covered, the best of which is that anti-marketing is the 'fundamentalist' arm of postmodernism – the bit that kicks convention where it hurts most.

It could also be loosely argued that anti-marketing is the practical application of postmodernist theory, a metamorphosis of traditional, modernist 'pull' marketing, given a 21st century digital twist, where the marketeer creates attraction to the online brand and lets the customer beat an enthusiastic path to his or her site, keenly waving plastic. There is no 'pushing' of the product onto a tired and suspicious public here. It is the total opposite.

And how to create this attraction? Well, with the novel array of anti-marketing tactics available such as principled selling, ethics or relationship-building, an atmosphere of trust and honesty can be attempted. And let's not forget that it is selling the experience that matters, not the product. Why? Because there is so much stuff out there which is virtually identical.

To be unique today is a non-starter. The only way to push yourself ahead of the rest is by offering a brilliant service - something which is far better than the rest. Whether it is by listening to the customer's every worry or problem before the sale, or by offering exemplary after-sales service (or both), this is the only way forward in the crowded market place of the digital age.

And now comes another contradiction

Anti-marketing has also been described in terms of a 'less is more' culture (Sinha and Foscht: *'Reverse-Psychology Marketing'* 2007). This is a world where less of everything for the customer is actually good business. Less information; less service; less choice; less segmentation and much less availability.

Prune everything back, cut away the complications and make it easier for the public to choose. A sort of puritanical route for customers to tread. The Ryanair, Aldi and Argos route.

Sinha and Foscht saw anti-marketing as a return to a more manageable age. Too much of anything in their eyes only leads to confusion, frustration and dilatoriness in the customers' buying habits. We have already said that the average customer has the memory attention of a goldfish and a very high boredom factor, so why complicate everything with such a huge and confusing array of choice, service and information?

Such an idea might have seemed suicidal in the age of mass marketing, but with the advent of the digital age, marketing people have begun to realise that offering a wealth of choice to the customer is not necessarily a productive thing. It has become a case of the bamboozled customer not being able to see the wood for the trees. So, cut back on choice, service and information. Just provide a few alternatives with limited information and the minimum service. Customers should then cease to be confused, breathe a sigh of relief and buy from the limited choice available.

Why is this so attractive? One reason. Pare everything back and businesses can cut costs quite dramatically. They can then can pass on breathtaking discounts to their customers. Hence, the £10 air trip to Paris or Barcelona, courtesy of Ryanair. Or the whole week's groceries at Lidl or Aldi for about a fifth of what it would have cost at Waitrose. At least, that is what Messrs Sinha and Foscht think.

Let's not forget the green factor

Having a company vision which does most of the above and then incorporates global welfare, help for the third world and saving the polar bear, will also place you well ahead of the competition. Money is not everything, although some critics would say that companies that advocate this state of moral nirvana, are the rich and powerful ones, which can afford to be ethical, nice and global-friendly. Or need to rebrand an image which looks dangerously 'anti-global' in today's society (e.g. petrol and oil companies).

Then there is the trust and honesty factor

Sir Richard Branson said that honesty, integrity, trust and respect served him well over the years and that without them, you cannot sustain long-term success.

Traditional marketing did not pay much attention to this. Getting the sale was the prime objective. Kill for the sale. Sell your grandmother for the sale. Read Sun-Tzu's *'Art of War'* and watch *'Glengarry Glen Ross'*. Forget customer care and after-sales service – it was unnecessary and a waste of time, energy and money. Just count your cash all the way to the bank and put a deposit down on that red Ferrari. David Tovey (*Principled Selling*, 2012) said that '*selling was a noble profession that got itself a bad name*.' It is easy to see why.

It might be argued that such factors as trust, honesty, after-sales service and customer-care are more important than anything today and that they are not really anti-marketing at all, because they have become normal mainstream marketing tactics due to necessity, rather than anything else.

A really final thought

Back in 2007, Sinha and Foscht, set out four factors, which looked at the customer and his or her attitude to marketing and the dangers that marketing people faced if they did not start thinking differently.

Over-marketing: there simply is too much advertising, too much fragmentation, too many discounts and unending sales. This inevitably has led to customer torpor and lack of interest.

Low-credibility: people just don't believe anything anymore. All businesses claim they are the best with the lowest prices, leading to 'rabbits in headlights' syndrome for baffled customers.

Information-overload: people nowadays are showered with information from the moment they open their eyes in the morning to the moment they turn the lights out at night. Information is everywhere - on phones, the television, computers, laptops, tablets, posters, billboards, food wrappers, clothes and on all our possessions. And it is being relentlessly pushed down our throat (or through our letterboxes), all the time. The obvious result is that we have become inured to it all. It is just white noise.

Customer boredom: linked to all of the above. People have seen it all before and generally walk without a second thought.

Anti-marketing is the new mainstream marketing

It could be argued that anti-marketing, in the form of 'pull' marketing, shackled to honesty, a friendly after-sales service and new sales techniques have given forward-thinking businesses a fresh appeal to a public that thinks it has seen it all before and is bored stiff by it all and more and more irritated by marketing intrusiveness.

And keeping customers sweet is the key to keeping them coming back for years to come.

Then there is 'word-of-mouth' recommendation – the jewel in the Internet crown. Having satisfied customers tell their friends NOT so much about your products, but about how great the experience was, is what the Internet is all about.

Customer satisfaction during and after the sales process is everything today. If you read most of the comments placed on Amazon, they are concerned not primarily with the product, but with the speed of delivery and the condition that the product arrived in, not to mention the packaging and even where the parcel was left (by the delivery man or woman).

The product matters very little now in the online sales process. Once a customer has decided (for example) on a *'Remington Titanium MS 1822 shaver'*, he will hunt around a little (maybe one or two sites), get bored and then return to Amazon to buy the thing, as I did recently. The next and most pressing issue is when the product is going to be delivered. Delivery has become the single-most important factor. We are back to 'speed' again as the vital ingredient. We all want our stuff as fast as possible. We did not ask for this initially, but it has become a prime and increasingly not so unique USP. We expect the stuff to be at our door within minutes, because that is the latest promise.

And now, suppliers and logistics companies are even looking at the possibility of drones delivering our products – thus speeding up the process even more, although, as one elderly member of the public pointed out on television recently, *"I can't see drones delivering my new fridge-freezer!"*

Marketing has become a subtle game of attraction, persuasion (by non-threatening means), total honesty, speed and impeccable after-sales service. It really is as simple as that. We can play around with various tactics, which we can then wrap up in some grand strategy of being friendly, honest and humorous, but what it all boils down to today is just being able to produce stuff quickly, sell it and then deliver it so fast that it makes your eyes water!

We can also slap lots of labels onto our strategies and give them pseudo-scientific names. We can dabble with self-referentiality', de-differentiation and anti-foundationalism to help explain this new way of marketing to customers in the digital age. We can play with our anti-funnels and 'conelessness' and not produce any matrices at all. We can also prove that black is most certainly not black… but just might be white in certain circumstances. And we can call it all postmodernist marketing or anti-marketing. We can make it a science. Or an art. Or a craft. Or a philosophy. Or even witchcraft or magic.

It is probably all of these… and none of them.

What we should all realise is that no matter what we believe, marketing is just a game which we will still all be discussing in a hundred years' time, probably in some Post-Digital-Proto-Quantum-Cosmic Age. And still without a clue as to what is going on and why the customer is such a slippery enigma.

Perhaps the artist, Damien Hirst, should be left with the final words, since his comments are pretty good, to the point, postmodern, very anti-marketing and sort of sums up the whole shooting-match.

"Fuck the customer. If you make great fucking art, fuck them. Fuck what they want. They'll buy what you fucking give them. If you're great, they'll buy it. If you're making great art, you don't have to think about the punters."

28. about the perpetrator

Adrian Liley was born in Manchester, UK, but lived most of his early life in Wellingborough, Northants, England. He now lives in a smallish terraced house in Bromley, Kent.

He has worked as an English language teacher in Tokyo, Riyadh, Doha, London and Ramsgate, amongst other exotic places and has marketed and sold English language courses in about sixty countries around the world for a variety of language schools for around 30 years. He started his own study-abroad agency in mainland China (*Asiaquest*) in 2003, which represented the interests of over 50 western institutions, including some universities (one of which was in the Maldives). He has worked as a marketing manager and head of sales in 5 UK companies and regularly gives talks, workshops and seminars on the world of anti-marketing. He recently began a new venture (*SuperCourses.co.uk*), which helps foreign students get the best deal possible for their English courses in the UK, whilst adhering strictly to the principles of postmodernist marketing.

In a varied and colourful life, Adrian has travelled on the Trans-Siberian railway (when it really was roughing it); smuggled alcohol in countries in the Middle East; got horribly drunk in the city of Taichung in Taiwan; swum in shark-infested seas off the coast of Brazil; coached, captained and played in his department's football team in Doha, Qatar, which won the cup two years running and was the Northants Open Under 18 Lawn Tennis Champion in 1974 (of this, he is extremely proud). He has been mugged three times, robbed six times, sacked twice, made redundant three times, walked away from his job four times, had his cameras stolen nine times and been shot at once.

He has also written 6 novels (*'The Marketeer Series'*), which look very loosely at crime in the world of marketing and sales in the English language industry. He now has his own website (adrianliley.com), which covers everything from postmodernism and anti-marketing to his dad's oil paintings and family history. There is also a blog, of course. Well, there would be, because everyone is doing that sort of thing, nowadays.

29. more intelligent people than me

Andrews, Iain (2015) **Postmodern marketing: is it dead or alive?**

Arnold, Chris (2009) **Ethical marketing and the new customer** (Wiley)

Baudrillard, J. (1994) **Simulacra & Simulation** (University of Michigan Press)

Baudrillard, J. (1998) **The Consumer Society** (Sage)

Borg, James (2010) **Persuasion** (Prentice Hall / Pearson)

Brown, Stephen (1995) **Postmodern Marketing** (Routledge)

Brown, Stephen (1998) **Postmodern marketing 2** (Routledge)

Brown, Stephen (2001), **"Torment Your Customers (They'll Love It)"** (Harvard Business Review 79, September, pp. 82-88)

Brown, Stephen (2001), **Marketing – The Retro Revolution** (Sage)

Brown, Stephen (2003), **Free Gift Inside!!** (Capstone)

Brown, Stephen (2006) **The Marketing Code** (Marshall Cavendish Business)

Brown, Stephen (2008) **Agents and Dealers** (Marshall Cavendish Limited)

Brown, Stephen (2009) **The Lost Logo** (Marshall Cavendish Business)

Brown, Stephen (2016) **Brands and Branding** (Sage)

Cardenas, Don. Cardenas, Tammy (2011) **Principled Selling** (Xlibris)

Cova, B. (1996) **'The postmodern explained to managers'** (Business)

Duncan, Kevin (2010) **Marketing Greatest Hits** (A&C Black)

Fill, Chris (2009 5th ed) **Marketing Communications** (Prentice Hall)

Firat, A. Fuat and Nikhilesh Dholakia (1998) **'Consuming People: From Political Economy to Theaters of Consumption'** (Routledge)

Firat, A. Fuat, Dholakia, Nikhilesh, and Venkatesh, Alladi, (1995), **'Marketing in a Postmodern World,'** European Journal of Marketing, Vol. 29, no. 1, 40-56.

Gitomer, Jeffrey (2003) **The Sales Bible** (Wiley)

Gladwell, Malcolm (2000), **The Tipping Point: How Little Things Can Make a Big Difference** (Little Brown)

Godin, Seth (2000) **Unleashing the Ideavirus** (Dobbs Ferry, NH, Do You Zoom Books)

Godin, Seth (2005) **Purple Cow** (Penguin)

Godin, Seth (2012) **All Marketers Tell Stories** (Penguin Random House)

Godin, Seth (2014) **What to do when it's your turn** (The Domino Project)

Godin, Seth (2015) **We are all weird. The Rise of Tribes and The End of Normal** (Portfolio)

Godin, Seth (2018) **This is Marketing** (Portfolio)

Goldstein, Noah. Martin, Steve J. Cialdini, Robert B. **YES! 50 Secrets from the science of persuasion** (Profile)

Greenberg, Paul (2010 4th ed) **CRM at the speed of light** (McGraw Hill)

Hall, Richard (2009) **Brilliant Marketing** (Pearson)

Hsieh, Tony (2010) **Delivering Happiness** (Business Plus)

Humphreys, Tony (1996) **The power of 'negative' thinking** (Newleaf)

Kennedy, Dan S. Zagula, Matt (2012) **NOBS Trust-Based Marketing** (Entrepreneur)

Klein, Naomi (2000) **No Logo: Taking Aim at the Brand Bullies** (Flamingo)

Kotler, Philip, Dipak C. Jain, and Suvit Maesincee (2002), **Marketing Moves: A New Approach to Profits, Growth, and Renewal** (Harvard Bus. School Press)

Kotler, Philip. Armstrong, Gary. Wong, Veronica, Saunders, John. (2008 5th ed) **Principles of Marketing** (Prentice Hall)

Krogerus, Michael and Tschappeler, Roman (2008) **The Decision Book** (Profile Books)

Leboff, Grant (2014) **Stickier Marketing** (Kogan Page)

Levitt, Stephen D and Dubner, Stephen J (2014) **Think like a Freak** (Penguin)

Lindstrom, Martin (2012) **Brandwashed** (Kogan Page)

Lyotard, Jean-Francois (1984) **The Postmodern Condition: A Report on Knowledge** (University of Minnesota)

Magloff, Lisa **Drawbacks of a SWOT Analysis** (smallbusiness.chron.com)

Middleton, Simon (2011) **What you need to know about marketing** (Capstone)

Morgan, Steve (2019) **Anti-Sell** (Independent)

Noel, Dr Hayden (2009) **Consumer Behaviour** (AVA Publishing)

Norem, Julie K (2001) **The positive power of negative thinking** (Basic Books)

O'Donohoe, Stephanie (1997) **"Raiding the Postmodern Pantry: Advertising Intertextuality and the Young Adult Audience"** (European Journal of Marketing, 31 (3/4), pp. 234-54)

Ostergaard, Per. Fitchett, James A. Jantzen Christian (1999) **On Appropriation and Singularisation: Two Consumption Processes** (Advances in Consumer Research Viloume 16, eds. Eric J. Arnould and Linda Scott, Provo, UT: Association for Consumer Research. Pages 405-409

Ries, Al. Trout, Jack. (1993) **The 22 Immutable Laws of Marketing** (Harper Collins)

Seidel, Michelle (2019) Review of: LaMarco. Nicky: **Alternatives to the SWOT Analysis** (smallbusiness.chron.com)

Sinha, Indrajit & Foscht Thomas (2007) **Reverse Psychology Marketing** (Palgrave Macmillan)

Solomon, Michael R. Bamossey, Gary. Askegaard Soren. Hogg, Margaret K (1999-2010) **Consumer Behavious: A European Perspective** (Prentice Hall)

Taleb, Nassim Nicholas (2012) **Anti-Fragile** (Allen Lane)

Toffler, Alvin (1980) **The Third Wave** (William Morrow)

Tovey, David (2012) **Principled Selling** (Kogan Page)

Valentin, Edward K (2005) **Away with SWOT Analysis. Use Defensive/Offensive Evaluation instead** (Journal of Applied Business Research, spring 2005)

Waddington, Tess (2013) **The gloves are off: the rise of anti-marketing** (marketing week.com) https://www.marketingweek.com/the-gloves-are-off-the-rise-of-anti-marketing/

Wallman, James (2013) **Stuffocation** (Penguin)

Woods, Caspian (2013) **The Devil's Advocate** (Pearson)

www.ingramcontent.com/pod-product-compliance
Lightning Source LLC
Chambersburg PA
CBHW060328200326
41519CB00011BA/1872